The Genesis of Urban Centers in the Ancient World

MICHAEL T. VOLLBACH

HAYDEN
HM
MᶜNEIL

Hayden-McNeil Sustainability

Hayden-McNeil's standard paper stock uses a minimum of 30% post-consumer waste. We offer higher % options by request, including a 100% recycled stock. Additionally, Hayden-McNeil Custom Digital provides authors with the opportunity to convert print products to a digital format. Hayden-McNeil is part of a larger sustainability initiative through Macmillan Higher Ed. Visit http://sustainability.macmillan.com to learn more.

Printed in the United States of America

10 9 8 7 6 5 4 3 2 1

ISBN 978-0-7380-6376-8

Hayden-McNeil Publishing
14903 Pilot Drive
Plymouth, MI 48170
www.hmpublishing.com

Vollbach 6376-8 F13

Table of Contents

Acknowledgements

The development of this book, although brief in nature, was certainly not an activity that can be dispersed without acknowledging a group of people that played an important role in its completion. There was a time that I never thought a great deal about the role of the city in history. This changed when I returned to college to earn a Master of Science degree in Geography. Through a great stroke of luck I found myself taking graduate classes under the auspices of Dr. Norman Tyler. His lectures about cities and his introduction to me of great authors that have spent entire careers thinking about how the city was shaped changed my academic life. Reading Lewis Mumford and Spiro Kostof made me think about why I wasn't teaching this important aspect of history to my own students.

I gratefully thank Norman Tyler for his encouragement to write this initial work and his additional time that he spent discussing urban development in the ancient world. His notes on my writing have been extremely instrumental in reaching a final manuscript. I also would be remiss if I did not point out the excellent education that Eastern Michigan University provided. I will always be indebted to the University and fond of all the memories and knowledge that were accrued in Strong Hall.

The atmosphere that my parents fostered throughout my life has also played an important role in this book's completion. My father, Frederick, and my late mother, Shirley, always made certain that our home was a place that embraced knowledge and learning and pushed the idea of formal and informal education constantly. Their support, and awe of education, has been a constant in my life, and has made me a better person.

There have been some real yeoman efforts put forth by some people in the final stages that cannot be overlooked. I have to thank everyone at Hayden-McNeil for their support, particularly my managing editor, Eric Gallippo. Last-minute editing advice came from Elaine Dopp and Shelly Szuba, who dutifully performed a task in expert detail. Shelly was also instrumental in drafting important sketches that are found throughout the book that help explain important concepts to readers.

In conclusion, I must spend a brief moment thanking the one person that made the writing and finishing of this book possible—my wife. Shelly has been the one person that has encouraged the finishing of this book more than anyone else. This book was nothing more than a heap of notes sitting in a file cabinet until she encouraged me to strike forward and write again. She has understood the sometimes craziness of my writing habits and endured the loneliness of my time away. Thanks, honey; it's finally done.

M.T.V.

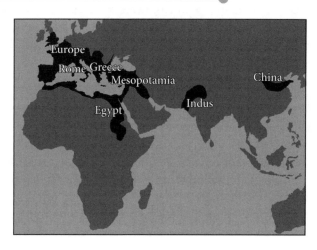

Introduction

The development of urban centers in the ancient world is rich and varied. Aristotle once wrote, "Men come to cities to live together, they remain in cities because they are unable to find a better way to exist." Throughout the history of urban civilization, mankind has come together to live for a variety of reasons. Often they converged together for safety against enemy intrusion; at other times aggregation occurred out of economic self-interest. Environment was also an important factor that forced congregation. As the world went through a warming trend at approximately 4,000 B.C.E., nomad bands followed animals to wetter regions where gathering and hunting became easier. The dynamics that brought people together is not as interesting as how men crafted their centers of living.

The emphasis of the research for this book has been placed on centers in seven civilizations that existed from 3,500 B.C.E. to 1,500 C.E. The seven civilizations chosen were found in Mesopotamia, Egypt, Indus, China, Greece, Rome, and Europe. Interest was focused on how each civilization's culture helped form its cities. This book was written with the intent of complementing a World Civilization course where students are attempting to understand the evolution of cities and how different cultural aspects impacted the development of those sites.

The need for students to become more acquainted with the evolution of urban centers is extremely important when studying World Civilization.

The word "civilization" finds its origin from the word *civitas*, Latin for city. So to adeptly study World Civilization, one is forced to know more about urban developments. In studying urban sites, one learns of the plethora of aspects that become decisive in its development.

Each chapter handles a unique civilization and reflects on four aspects of cultures that became decisive in urban development. First, the influence of religion on the development of the urban center will be discussed. The need for cult centers and the influence of the priesthood are important in shaping cities. Early civilizations came into existence with a government that can best be termed as a theocracy. The importance of the priesthood could affect how the city was shaped. Often, the location of worship centers had a major effect on how the rest of the center was formed. It also impacted the residential patterns in some civilizations.

Following religion, economics will be discussed. Although all major civilizations discussed will be agrarian or pastoral in nature, each will reach a point when trade is important. Location of trade routes, such as superhighways, will shape cities. The need to develop areas in cities where trade becomes paramount, like the marketplace, is not uniform in each civilization. Among the Greeks and the Romans the marketplace was known as the agora, an important place not only for trade, but also as a central meeting place where political matters were discussed. Contrary to this was the Chinese market that was deemed unimportant in early planned cities. Each civilization took their own approach to trade and where it should be conducted, but the act of trade impacted the shape of the city nonetheless. Trade centers in the center of the city will seem the norm in some areas, while centers tied to religious sites or near bodies of water become the rule in others. Understanding the differences in economic development assists in understanding the people of the civilization better.

Often, religion and economics leads to the feature of militarism that shapes many cities. Many early civilizations discovered the need for city walls and citadels, although not immediately. Often, walls and citadels are a manifestation of what each civilization finds most important. Should the temple be guarded? Should all cities be guarded? Should economic centers be protected in this manner as well? The answers to all these questions will vary and will disclose the importance of each characteristic of the urban centers studied. Militarism is not solely limited to the building of walls and citadels. In fact, the absence of such items sheds a great deal of light on how a civilization evolved as well. The discussion of standing armies or the decision to maintain an army of citizen soldiers is also of interest in the shaping of cities.

Philosophy, although directly tied to religion in some civilizations, often reflects general attitudes of the people. These general attitudes mirror the outlook of the civilization and how they shaped their urban sites. If the student of history simply boiled the philosophy of the civilization down to whether their philosophy was generally positive or negative, a better understanding of why the urban site was built in a certain manner could be acquired. These general attitudes are found in ancient literature, law codes, and religious documents. All primary documents are open for interpretation in this manner.

All cities, whether ancient or current, have either formed organically or were planned. Simply put, an organic city is a center that was unplanned and grew as citizens expanded a given area. A planned city is exactly what the word suggests—a site that a person or group of people designed before they began building. The discussion of whether the major cities fit in one category or another will also be addressed in each chapter. Arguably, one could say that every city has some planning involved. The idea of building near arable land might have involved planning, but the planning may have ended there. Many urban sites had planners that truly conceptualized where specific classes would live, where people would worship, and where trade would take place. Streets were also laid out with specific details in width and breadth. Many planners thought out the development of sewage systems and how to transport clean water to the center of the city. Planning was normally the result of a ruler that had a specific vision or was interested in self-aggrandizement. Whatever the reason, planners and their role in the evolution of the urban matrix were important.

All of the above aspects will be examined in detail. The goal of this book is that students of World Civilization will develop a better understanding of the complexity that existed behind ancient urban centers and how cultures duly effected their growth. The hope is that an additional layer of understanding of the ancient world is offered to those interested in the shape of the urban center.

x

CHAPTER 1

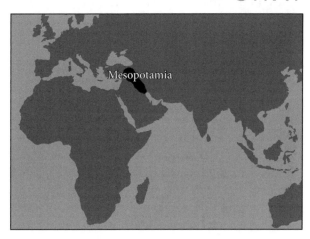

Mesopotamia

The story of ancient civilizations and the first urban centers that evolved is centered in Mesopotamia. Mesopotamia is often labeled as "the land of firsts," so it is no surprise that we see urbanization in a civilization take place here before any other area of the world. Often there is discussion asking why here and not Egypt, Harappa, or any other place in the world? The answer is simple. Geography and climate forced the people of the Fertile Crescent to live and work together, forming the first cities that led to the first civilization.

During the Paleolithic Age, man was nomadic, sustaining themselves through hunting and gathering. These activities were gender specific, but both activities had something in common. A land could be over-hunted and over-gathered. When this occurred, the band of nomads, which might have amounted to no more than 50 to 100 people, would move on to greener pastures to graze. Finding those new pastures involved following herds of animals and at least temporarily settling where fresh water and food were found. Archaeological evidence suggests that men began to settle around the Fertile Crescent, an expansive area that is bounded by the Tigris and Euphrates Rivers, to hunt and gather over 6,000 years ago. This productive land encouraged men to dispense with nomadic life, and by the Neolithic Age, man had become sedentary throughout Mesopotamia. The climate change that was evidenced by 4,000 B.C.E. made the Earth considerably warmer, and may have forced migration toward river valleys such as the Fertile

Crescent. A significant flood that took place to the north of the Fertile Crescent, forming the area known as the Black Sea, also may have given some impetus to a migration further south.

Historians disagree how agrarianism took hold, but there are several good theories regarding its beginnings. Some think it was an attempt to control the masses. Others argue that man turned to farming as an alternative to the hunting and gathering that nomadic life constantly entailed. The major theory that is supported today, though, is that gatherers of the community found that the indiscriminate seed that may have been dropped during their daily chores led to the growth of the plant at a later date. Realizing this phenomenon made gathering easier. Shortly after realizing this, gatherers began throwing seeds on the ground with the hopes that they would not have to travel so far in the future for grain and other foodstuff. This would support the sedentary lifestyle of man. Hunting and fishing would continue, but early domestication of plants would dominate man's life and support their success. Domestication of animals, outside of dogs, would soon follow, and man would have no reason to leave their new homes.

The development of villages during the Neolithic Age would eventually give rise to urban life. In Mesopotamia, that transformation first saw a period where smaller villages found it necessary to work together with other smaller villages for geographical and environmental reasons. The greatest environmental challenge that Mesopotamians faced in the southern section was the flooding of the rivers. Flooding took place in both the northern and southern section of Mesopotamia but, because the Tigris and the Euphrates rivers meet in the south before they empty into the Persian Gulf, flooding was much more pervasive in that area.

Although flooding was more significant in the south, it must be realized that it was this flooding that brought them to settle. Settlement took place because men were initially following animals that came to the region for the fresh water and abundant crop to feed off of year round. Later, settlement became permanent when this silty plain provided a fertile soil necessary for farming, thus sustaining the village. The flooding provided silt not only from local river beds but from the accumulation of silt that was pushed down the rivers. However, the flooding could wipe out crops, destroy homes and villages, and cause the deaths of locals. The need to control the flooding led to mass engineering projects that could control floods through irrigation.

Floods came under better control when swamps were drained and irrigation efforts were organized to handle the enormous flooding that the area experienced. Both activities required a massive amount of cooperation⌊ The village, at an early stage, learned that cooperation would lead to future success, as fields became greener and animals were raised more successfully when the waters were under control. When floods became controlled locally, villages increased in size and began farming larger expanses of land. This brought them in contact with other local villages, often forming larger villages where further irrigation projects were worked on for their mutual benefit and walls were built as a form of protection against outsiders and environmental disasters.⌉

These early villages would eventually lead to a point where cult centers would be born. Early villages were theocracies. These governments, led by priests, had worship centers within the villages. Prior to 3,500 B.C.E., cult centers were developed outside the boundaries of the village. Such cult centers were not true cities, but places of worship and pilgrimages. They may initially have had no resident populations, but they became the place where cities crystallized. The cult center became known in Mesopotamia as the temenos, or religious precinct. The temenos had a variety of buildings within it, but nothing was of greater importance than the ziggurat.

It is the ziggurat, the Mesopotamian monument to the gods, that provides such centers a later urban existence (Figure 1.1). Living on the

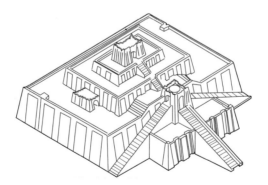

Figure 1.1 The Ziggurat of Ur-Nammu: The ziggurat was the center of newly founded cult centers. Here priests honored the many gods of the Mesopotamian religion and gave sacrifice. The picture above is an artist's rendering of the Ziggurat of Ur-Nammu. This massive step pyramid measured 210 feet in length, 150 feet in width, and over 100 feet in height. (Based on an illustration by Shelly Szuba.)

alluvial plains of lower Mesopotamia, residents built these terraced pyramids as a reminder of earlier lives. Many residents of southern Mesopotamia came from other areas where worshipping of gods took place at high elevations, such as mountains and plateaus. Living in the south meant there were no physical characteristics that could be used to worship their gods. Mountains needed to be built, and the ziggurats provided Mesopotamians with their mountains. Normally walled off, the temenos offered one of the few places where open air existed within in the later city (Figure 1.2). Although urban centers had a tendency to

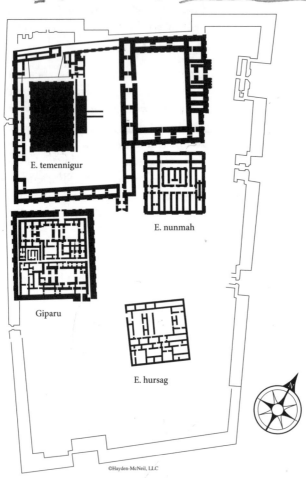

E. temennigur

E. nunmah

Giparu

E. hursag

©Hayden-McNeil, LLC

Figure 1.2 The Temenos: The temenos (E. Temennigur) in early Babylon, which can be found in the northeast section of the city, had a wall surrounding the cult center. As the population surrounding the temenos grew, additional buildings were built, such as the Giparu, an area where the priestess was housed; E. Hursag, an additional building of worship, meant "house of the mountains;" and E. Nunmah, the "house of the exalted prince." This illustrates the impact that the initial temenos had on the growth of the city.

affiliate themselves with one major god, this did not preclude the worship of others. In Nebuchadnezzar's Babylon (604–562 B.C.E.), the cult of Marduk dominated the culture and was personified in the dominating ziggurat named Etemenanki. But Babylon also boasted 43 cult centers of the great gods of Babylon, 300 chapels or "holy places" of the Igigi, 600 chapels of the Nunnaki, 180 open air shrines, and 202 various cult stations.

Early temenos were built on non-arable land. In a community in which success was based primarily on the consequences of their multiple agrarian harvests, the use of arable land for the building of a cult center would have been unconscionable. The primary importance for all Mesopotamians would be to use all arable land to its utmost. Mesopotamian civilization was agrarian in nature, and it is fair to say that every family in this early culture gleaned their existence in this manner at some time. There were arguably two major seasons in the year for these people: the dry season and the wet season. The dry season involved farming, of which there were two harvests throughout the year. The wet season could be prolonged. It would not be long until more successful farmers gravitated toward cult centers during the wet season. Not much work could be done on one's land during the wet season, so second homes were built outside the walls of the temenos by the wealthy. The rule of thumb was: the closer your second home was to the temenos, the more important you were. These second homes amounted to nothing more than townhouses, but they added much to the evolution of the first urban sites in the world. Such cities as Eridu, Ur, Larsa, and Uruk trace their genesis to agrarian people that eventually congregated near religious centers.

Early sites were made up of owners of larger estates that had improved their lives through the positioning of their land near less frequent flood hazard zones. This enabled fewer losses while still being near a canal that offered them the life-giving forces of one of the major rivers or tributaries that still offered success. These estate owners would have attained enough prominence to have possessed slaves and other workers to keep them in the status equal to that of an important lord of the land.

As these Mesopotamian cultures evolved from subsistence farmers to a civilization that developed agrarian surplus, the population grew. Naturally, people continued to congregate near cult centers, and eventually this formed the basis for populations large enough to be termed cities.

These early cities contained residences, temples, and a palace that was typically walled off. An outer city or suburb contained an agglomeration of housing, farms, gardens, and pastures. It is quite evident that cult centers helped shape the early Mesopotamian cities. Although no given order seemed apparent in their development, all Mesopotamians seemed to find a connection with religion. Sir C. Leonard Woolley argued, "Every feature of the early city revealed the belief that man was created for no other purpose than to magnify and serve his gods. That was the city's ultimate reason for existence."

The initial temenos featured a wall to protect it from outsiders, but as well-to-do farmers built near the cult center, other walls were built so as to protect themselves. Later, more walls were built to protect their second homes. The net result is that the cult center was the seed of an urban sprawl that would take place throughout Mesopotamia. It was in these southern sites, circa 3,500 B.C.E., that large-scale monument building, the tradition of writing, and large population came together to form the civilization. It is important to note that although an enclosed wall seems to have been the rule, there were exceptions. Outside the city wall was a special sanctuary called the New Year's Chapel. Once a year, the image of the main deity of the city was carried out in a procession accompanied by worshippers. A sacred road was built for this procession. Although we do not know why the sanctuary was outside of the wall, one can see the beginning of road building outside of the main urban setting.

Religion developed the city into three major sections. Initially we see this only in Sumerian sites, but future sites to the north have similarities. The city proper (libbi ali) was the oldest section of the city. This originated with a temenos and temples, the palace and administrative centers, residences of royal officials, and the houses of citizens. This area was walled at an early stage and was administered from the gates where the mayor conducted his business. The next area was a suburb (uru bar ra), or outer city. Here we find a mixture of houses, agrarian activity, pastoralism, and small gardens. It can be argued that the development of the suburb took place primarily because the city proper, which found its origin in the religious precinct, was formed and suburbs were the next natural step. Finally there was a financial district known as the karu. Each district finds its origin in religion. Had the temenos not formed, the city proper would not have grown around its walls, the suburb would not have been created, and a financial district would not have arisen to further develop city life.

Just as religion was an important cultural determinant in the development of early Mesopotamian cities, economics also played a vital role in those same urban centers. Every city possessed a harbor area, or karu, which served as the center for commercial activity. The karu existed outside the city proper and its suburb, and its merchants enjoyed administrative independence and the separate legal status important for citizens transacting business there (Figure 1.3). In the karu were

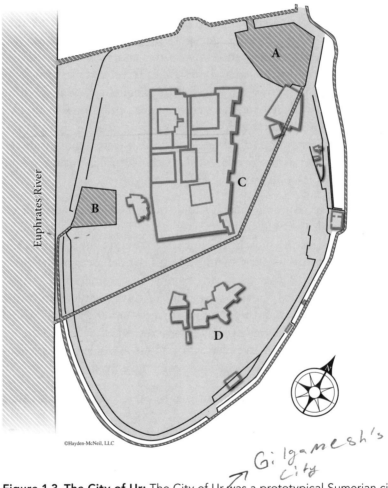

©Hayden-McNeil, LLC

Gilgamesh's City

Figure 1.3 The City of Ur: The City of Ur was a prototypical Sumerian city that evolved from a cult center to a profitable merchant site. Sections A and B on the maps were karus where merchants conducted a great deal of their trade and lived not far from the area. Note that both harbors were man-made and were controlled by small entries to deter unwanted guests. Section C on the map denotes where the original temenos expanded, and section D marks where further settlement took place.

stores, taverns, and residences of foreign traders. Administrative independence was important as foreigners received different rights in the karu than they did in other areas of the city. The merchants of the karu relied heavily on water routes to conduct their business. The river systems were often supplemented by canals that were built. Trade centers usually did not emerge outside of river systems. Confining trade activities of an economic nature to this area of the city assisted in the early development of most Mesopotamian cities.

River systems dominated the way in which trade took place, but they did not exclude other forms of transport. Overland trade was also important in Mesopotamian economics. Overland trade began in the karu, but it never dominated as a method of travel because roads outside of the city proper were not well kept. Frequent flooding and the lack of drainage made overland trade a viable option only in the dry season. Also, overland trade could become dangerous in times of political and military upheaval. When paved roads were built outside the city proper, not only did overland trade become easier, but the sphere of influence of the city was extended.

Not all of the economic activity took place outside the city proper. Markets also existed inside the walled section of the city. Lewis Mumford suggests that early markets were found in the temenos, and only at a later date would they move to residential areas of the cities. Mumford's assertion seems to ring true when considering that most Mesopotamian cities evolved organically. With first settlement taking place near complexes, it seems logical that a market economy would soon follow. As residential districts grew and temples became more reserved for the few, the market center had to move to a less conspicuous place—normally the area where common people lived.

In this area, a free town market thrived. Local artisans and craftsmen, along with merchants traveling from city to city, plied their wares in return for payment in kind or a disk of silver that acted as money. The idea of supply markets with permanent shops was a late development in Mesopotamian cities and was probably stimulated by the growth of the center. These market areas found themselves situated near gates that evidently linked those living outside the city with those living inside the city. The belief that some of these markets were once periodic and served the needs of those who first settled near the temenos is undoubtedly true.

Lewis Mumford asserts in *The City in History*, "What gives the market a permanent place in the city is a population big enough to offer a handsome living to merchants with distant connections and costly commodities, and sufficient local productivity to enable the surplus of urban workshops to be offered in general sale. But these conditions are a result, not an original cause, of the growth of population." By making this last statement, Mumford is claiming that economics did not play a major role in population growth. Rather, Mumford claims that dynamic changes in climate forced people to live closer together, which is not entirely correct. Although it is well known that climate changes did force migration throughout the world, Mumford's statement flies in the face of the generally accepted thesis that surplus agriculture allowed men to seek out other endeavors. Certainly some of these endeavors involved early trade through barter. As civilization became more diverse, it was a natural progression to see settlement sizes increase in a given area due to the fact that more was offered within their burgeoning centers. The locations of cities such as those in southern Mesopotamia attracted people bent on making a living in a rich cultural setting that controlled the Persian Gulf. A market settlement evolution attracted people. Economics caused population to grow.

With this population growth came a by-product of the market: writing. Early Mesopotamians found it important to communicate the results of a transaction. This simple communication first involved cylindrical seals that marked an image of a person who played a role in the transaction. Cylindrical seals soon gave way to cuneiform, a form of writing that required a wedge-shaped (cunei) stylus to write on clay tablets. This writing quickly moved Mesopotamians from pictography to logograms to phonography. Writing was important because it offered another aspect to the market that helped develop a successful city.

Although writing was important, true success and prosperity economically came when a strongman or king had become triumphant. Defeating and subjugating a neighbor was important to the economy because it brought tribute and the spoils of war back to the city. This initially made the ruler and the elite very wealthy, but that wealth would trickle down the socioeconomic stations so the city in general reaped the glory of the conqueror. Roads were built, for military reasons, during these military high points, which would later serve as trade routes where merchants could then travel from city to city. This would add to the success and growth of cities, although it should be noted that these periods of success were not always constant and it was during these low points that the economy declined dramatically.

The physical result of economics is fourfold. First, as was already mentioned, population grew as a result of economics. Second, a new section of the city called the karu became important. Not only did water routes and overland trade begin there, thus becoming the center of commercial activity, but it also became a place where foreign traders lived. The karu also existed as a place where foreign traders kept stores and factories. But it must be remembered that the karu existed outside the city proper that was normally walled. Third, economics brought to Mesopotamia further social stratification. This stratification was displayed through the building of private housing by well-to-do citizens inside the city proper, some who had become successful through economic endeavors. Finally, military success led to the building of roads that assisted in developing trade abroad and a boost in the economy that was evident throughout all economic classes.

Although religion can be seen as an early determinant that shaped the Mesopotamian city and economics as a source that developed the center further, nothing affected their progress more than militarism. Ancient Mesopotamian history is marked with constant warfare. The location of this fertile land, which offered few natural defenses from foreign intruders, virtually invited any group that was so inclined to invade the area. As climate changed and the surrounding area began to dry, the migration of peoples found themselves pushing into the more successful area of Mesopotamia. Sometimes an organized incursion took place, but more often it was unorganized and less obvious. Whatever the case, Mesopotamians were constantly faced with new groups that wanted the same thing Mesopotamians possessed—a more stable existence. Later, when empires form, that desire for stability will be replaced with the aspiration of expansion into that same area.

The litany of invasions that took place throughout the history of Mesopotamia is extensive and is of less importance to this research than are the effects frequent attacks and the reaction the residents had on those incidents. Those reactions led to a striking change of cities. The early cult centers that later evolved into the urban centers of Mesopotamia were first occupied by successful farmers and sometimes by conquerors. With invasion always an issue at hand, the presence of walls became a feature of most cities. Initial walls surrounded only temple complexes, leaving the palace and residential sections exposed. Later, cities to the north began the practice of enclosing the entire urban unit (Figure 1.4). As well, the citadels that were once located in the center of urban sites in early centers soon straddled walls during later periods.

©Hayden-McNeil, LLC

Figure 1.4 The Enclosed City of Babylon: The enclosure of the entire urban unit was atypical and was found in the north first. Babylon is a prime
example of this enclosure taking place. Notice the origin of Babylon can be
seen in the rectangular layout in the east side of the Euphrates River; further
expansion was much more planned with rectilinear streets.

As warfare became more complex and siege warfare was introduced,
an outer wall was often built with towers and complicated gates. Walls
became the dominant feature of Mesopotamian architecture, along
with the construction of elaborate gates. These walls and gates not
only fulfilled the obvious need for defense, but also acted as a way for
kings to display their wealth and magnificence. Walls demonstrated
whether the king was proficient in his job. The worst thing that could
be said about a king, as was mentioned of Gilgamesh of Uruk, was
that "he did not keep good walls." Fortunately for the citizens of Uruk,
Gilgamesh changed his ways and began to keep "good walls." It was
only then that he was revered as a great king.

In cities like Nebuchadnezzar's Babylon, which is most noted for
its hanging gardens, it is his constant work on the city's walls that
should not go unnoticed. Nebuchadnezzar spent a good deal of time,
money, and energy in rebuilding and fortifying existing walls. His city
proper had a triple wall, perhaps re-emphasizing his war-like nature.
The walls were an impressive 40 feet tall and were wide enough to
allow chariots to race. At one point, Nebuchadnezzar even changed
the shape of the city by diverting a river and building the Western
Outlook (Figure 1.5). This change further articulated his greatness.

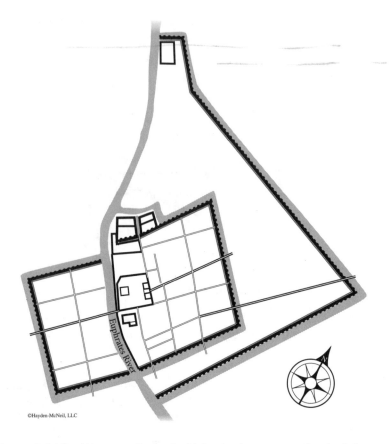

©Hayden-McNeil, LLC

Figure 1.5 The Western Outlook: Nebuchadnezzar was fond of demonstrating his power through building projects. The Western Outlook project enlarged a section of the city, built additional walls, and diverted the Euphrates River.

Nebuchadnezzar was a perfect example of a warrior-king who was successful militarily and whose success was reflected in his city. His victories abroad meant that he would have the necessary tribute, materials, and skilled and unskilled laborers, through prisoners of war, to create this magnificent city. Nebuchadnezzar is remembered in the Old Testament as the King that defeated Judah and deported 10,000 craftsmen and artisans for the express purpose of using their skills for building projects. It was only when a Mesopotamian city had a victorious king in their palace that the center could rise above mere subsistence. The spoils of war, as well as tribute, raised the standard of living for soldiers, bureaucrats, and workers alike. Temples and palaces were built, or in some cases rebuilt, with metals and timber abroad. In essence, military might mean that cities were offered new urban life and became enriched and vital.

Militarism, or at least the increasing importance of it, also affected the layout of cities and street design. As mentioned earlier, early Mesopotamian cities formed organically with no specific street layout that could be labeled. With the advent of large scale military power, the arrangement of the street, temple, and palace would become a necessary consideration. The maps of early cities show the temple and palace separate, often with the temple walled off from the rest of the city. Later layouts reflect temples and palaces as one unit in some centers, possibly reflecting the role of the king as the high priest. The position of the citadel also changed with the congregation of the palace and the temple. Early cities had citadels positioned in their center, perhaps for two reasons. One, central location allowed those in power a vantage point to better control the masses. Two, central locations were reminiscent of military encampments. Some northern Mesopotamian cities reflected this layout, often with either a rectangular or round city plan, while southern Mesopotamian cities often had ovaloid shapes. Northern Mesopotamian cities reflect these early encampments in that the royal tent was consistently placed off-center with the sacred standards. Later, northern planned towns found the royal citadel, palace, and temple in a similar layout. In the south, the king was positioned in the most protected area. When the palace and temple did congregate, the citadel always moved with them to a raised position on the ramparts.

Less is known about street arrangements, although the city of Ur throws some light on the issue. Its streets included standardized widths and rectangular crossings, with few unpredictable turns. This uniformity of streets, particularly in later cities, suggests the need to move an army effortlessly through the streets.

Royal roads were built with the intent to control conquered territories. The idea was to make sure that past enemies did not rise up against the victors. These roads were important to maintain. Disrepair such as grass growing on the royal path meant that economic and military collapse was at hand. Nineveh, like many significant cities, established a royal road for returning armies. Its width was of legal importance; anyone building a house along the road that encroached upon it could be punished by death.

Not only did the walls that were built offer the necessary defense from enemies, they also offered religious unification and control over the masses, and created a sharp delineation between that which was urban and that which was country. Although some agrarianism and pastoralism was found within the city, the country offered a vast amount of agricultural land that was divided by the walled boundaries of the city. But the walls in ancient Mesopotamia were, more than any other feature, the most dominant characteristic of the city. The importance of the city could be discerned by simply looking at these man-made borders. This monumental building was protected by their deities and given long names.

The gateways that accompanied these walls often served as civic centers. Much of the business of state would take place at these gateways, and many administrators met here on official business. Gateways were also used as a place where the ruler would situate a military base and perhaps remind citizens of his might by erecting a statue of himself. Gateways belonged to city quarters where unique activities such as fish selling or metallurgy took place nearby. This military gateway gave way to some unique markets, although this should not be confused with the standard open-air market of the ancient city. The entrance of the city was carefully controlled—so much so that very few came in and out of the urban site daily. This meant there was not a great deal of congestion near the gates until later periods.

Gates of cities were symbolically reinforced by threatening bulls or lions, huge magic images of deified power. Mesopotamians thought these images would dissuade oncoming armies and impress visitors of their supremacy. The ramparts had towers and citadels developed with walls so thick that counter-weapons could be used from above. Walls became so complicated that intrigue was more likely than protracted siege warfare to make them fall. To many, these complicated walls were not only a statement of their own urban center's greatness but also the greatness of their gods, to whom the walls were dedicated upon their building. In *The Epic of Gilgamesh*, a perfect example of the importance of the walls is articulated in this discussion of the main character building the wall of Uruk:

"Of ramparted Uruk the wall he built;
Of hallowed Eanna the pure sanctuary.
Behold its outer wall, whose cornice is like copper,
Peer at the inner wall, which none can equal!
Seize upon the threshold, which is of old.
Go up and walk on the walls of Uruk,
Inspect the base terrace, examine the brickwork:
Is not its brickwork of burnt brick?
Did not the Seven Sages lay its foundations?"

In Ancient Mesopotamia, the construction of the city wall did not only shape the urban site, but it also had a bearing as to whether the king was proficient as a ruler. To say that a ruler kept "good walls" was an important accolade that every king wished to possess. If a ruler kept "bad walls," then they were unable to protect their residents from foreign incursions and likely natural disasters. The city took shape through the military. The shape was of the utmost importance to the people and to the king who ruled the center. The shape was an enunciation of the importance of the people, their gods, and their king.

The general philosophy of Mesopotamians would also have an effect on the urban center's development, although its effect was not as rich as later civilizations. Mesopotamian philosophy, which finds its roots in their religion and can be studied through their literature, is at best negative. This negative philosophy is born from the environment in which they lived. Living in a land where oppressive heat and unpredictable floods could ruin a crop at any time certainly must have affected their belief system. As well, reoccurring foreign invasions kept this civilization from claiming any "chosen people" status. The major piece of literature for this civilization, *The Epic of Gilgamesh*, gives even better understanding of their philosophy.

In the epic, Gilgamesh, a historic king, learns that the afterlife is not a cheery place to aspire to upon death. No heaven entered into the belief system of these people. No matter how righteous you are on Earth, you are quarantined in the afterlife with the least favorable for eternity. Together you are joined in a house of dust and clay. This convinces Mesopotamians to live their mortal lives in a judicious manner and become worthy followers of the gods. This important subservice needed to take place because the gods of the Mesopotamians were a capricious lot. Collectively, these gods decided to wipe out mankind for being nothing more than boisterous. This capriciousness led the Mesopotamians to develop a philosophy that further shaped their cities.

Every civilization develops a philosophy behind how they will relate to their god(s). This relationship with the divine could fall anywhere from loving to harsh. The Mesopotamians, particularly the early Sumerians, felt that they were put on this Earth to serve their gods and the relationship was not loving. Every Mesopotamian was familiar with a man named Utnapishtim, who was selected by one god to survive with others by building an ark and riding out the divine flood that will wipe out the rest of the world. The story of this flood is found in *The Epic of Gilgamesh*. The main character Gilgamesh, hoping to avoid death, spends the entire epic seeking everlasting life to no avail. Not only do Mesopotamians have little to look forward to in their harsh world, they have less to look forward to in the next world. The lesson learned? Live your life to the fullest. As the goddess Siduri tells Gilgamesh, "Man was born to die. So put on the clean clothes, embrace your wife and clasp the child's hand, for you too will die."

The essential messages mentioned above in *The Epic of Gilgamesh* affected urban development. It is obvious that Mesopotamians took great pains to please their sometimes vengeful gods. These ancient urbanites believed that they were created to please the gods. Thus, the building of early cult centers and the later importance placed on the temenos are natural. Early cooperation was also an important outgrowth of their philosophy. Living in such an environmentally challenged area, the building of canals and walls must simply have been an attempt to live life to the fullest by making their surroundings more hospitable.

It is difficult to say whether their approach to housing structure might also be an attempt to live to the fullest, as those with wealth seemed inclined to live in similar-sized homes as other residents. The goal in building a home was comfort, particularly from the sun and other elements. This accounts for the one and two-story buildings with no windows. It was the development of great urban centers like Babylon that reflected Nebuchadnezzar's attempt to enjoy life while he could. Not even kings enjoyed heavenly status in the afterlife and as great kings knew of this, they made as much of their mortal life as possible. This meant bawdy cities were built, sometimes with slave labor, for the world to remember. One should not be surprised that the Hanging Gardens, the Tower of Babel, and the Great Walls of Babylon fascinated both the ancients and the contemporaries.

Four factors have been examined as decisive determinants in the development of urban centers. But no discussion on cities would be complete without reviewing the role of planners. Early cult centers had no official planners. A.E.J. Morris describes this early growth as organic, or uncontrolled. Although most of the cities in ancient Mesopotamia seemed organic, city plans, as was mentioned earlier, mirrored early military encampments. Rectangular and round city plans have military encampments as their prototypes. Assyrian reliefs of these plans can be seen as possible early plans that were the foundations of later cities. Although this may be true, the walling off of temple complexes seems to suggest the beginnings of urban planning. With the advent of strongmen and kings, other considerations were made in regards to the city proper that must have been termed "planned." By the third millennium B.C.E., almost all cities had walls. The temenos became an official separate district in the city proper, while the karu appeared as a standard outside of the city. The development of walls suggests those that were doing the planning were high-level bureaucrats or military men. Large cities that were dominated by warrior-kings became interested not only in defense but also wanted to stay in the good graces of the gods, thus more temples. As well, public works projects became a method in which self-aggrandizement took place. Our ancient planners in Mesopotamia evolved from religious roots, to strongmen, to warrior-kings.

● CHAPTER 2

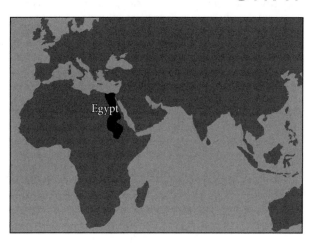

EGYPT

While Mesopotamia was developing history's first civilization and earliest urban centers, Egypt was soon becoming a culture that would be unrivaled in the ancient world. By 3,100 B.C.E., Egypt would be united following a series of civil wars. The history of this is so unreliable that often the unification is attributed to a legendary strongman by the name of Menes, while in other accounts a king named Narmer is credited to this development. It is more probable that a series of rulers united Egypt and began to impose a dynastic rule that would help develop this river valley into a complex civilization that remained relevant throughout Roman world dominance and beyond.

In many ways, Egypt and Mesopotamia were similar. Both were set in river valleys and relied heavily on the flooding of their primary rivers to create fertile farming. Both were beset with marshy deltas and desert regions. But similarities between the two, particularly when considering urbanization, end there.

Part of the reason Egypt formed as a civilization so much later than Mesopotamia rests on the fact that its geographic location kept it safe from reoccurring foreign intrusions. This allowed the Egyptians the ability to concentrate less on defenses and more on their precious religious centers and necropolises. Anyone that has become mildly intimate with Ancient Egypt is familiar with the pyramids that were built to entomb pharaohs and other important family members. An extraordinary amount of time was spent building shrines and tombs during each kingdom, particularly during the Old Kingdom. In order to build these monuments, vast resources were tapped. It has been suggested that the use of these resources was one reason early cities were not more permanent. So much emphasis was put on the building materials for tombs that cities were left to be made of mud-brick.

The earliest known example of city planning dates back to the city of Kahun. The city was of considerable size and was intended for the workmen building the pyramid of Senwosret II. There was a wall that surrounded the city; its purpose was probably more to keep laborers in than to keep intruders out. The city itself was divided internally by a wall. On the east side of the city were the houses of the chief people and better-class workers; the west side housed the lower-class workers (Figure 2.1). They lived there until the death and burial of the king, and then, as there was no more work, they drifted elsewhere and the houses fell into disrepair. The plan of the streets was gridiron with a main street 180 feet wide. Lewis Mumford suggests that the size of this main street is religiously motivated, as it was probably used as a processional way. As well, the argument is presented that gridiron plans were used because they were simple. Because these worker cities needed to be put up quickly, an organic pattern was not logical.

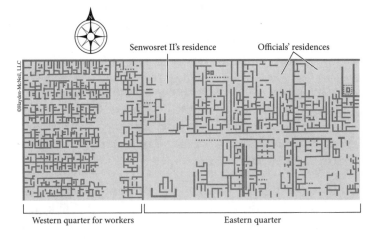

Figure 2.1 The City of Kahun: The city of Kahun, also known as Lahun, was a rectangular planned settlement measuring about a third of a mile by half of a mile. Kahun is an example of a planned city that reached a population of 3,000. Residents busied themselves with the building of the pyramid of Senwosret II. As can be seen, lower-class workers resided in the western quarter.

Another prime example of the temporary city was Tel-el-Amarna. Its founder, Akhenaten (ca. 1,379–1,362 B.C.E.), preserved a special spot for himself in world history. In a fiercely polytheistic society, Akhenaten introduced the first monotheistic religion in Egypt, the cult of Aten. As pharaoh, he decided to build a new city, Akhetaten (Tel-el-Amarna), that was laden with religious symbolism and was removed from the polytheistic Thebes. Unlike Kahun, Akhetaten was a royal city. Essentially this meant that the pharaoh took up permanent residence with the offices of a substantial part of the government. There was normally more than one royal city; the size of Egypt necessitated administrative bodies in two places, normally Thebes and Memphis. The presence of Akhetaten offered a third royal city during his reign.

The innovation of Akhetaten should not be surprising, as Akhenaten was an innovative man. The city reveals the symbolism of this new monotheistic sun cult and the utilitarian nature that lies behind a royal city. Akhetaten was situated on a plain that was dominated by hills in the east. In a cult centered on the sun, the significance of the sun rising over the hills to shine on the city must have been important. The agricultural land on the opposite bank was defined strictly by the projection of the sun.

The city of Akhetaten was laid out with utilitarian functions, as well as symbolic needs in mind. The city had a ribbon-like pattern along the Nile, with royal residences and a bureaucratic office to the north. The major cult place fell to the south (Figure 2.2). The workers' residences were laid out to the east. Burial places were symbolic, with the royal family tomb set on the horizon. Although Akhetaten was certainly planned, the housing of the "service population," outside the central zone, was not. Thus the long-term effect on the workers' residences was organic.

Both Kahun and Akhetaten are examples of cities that formed during a Pharaoh's reign and, after his death, converted to a religious complex maintained by priests. Workers in Akhetaten, like Kahun, lived in mundane buildings. The living quarters were quite standardized and built with impermanence in mind. Although it may not have been built for the ages, it is important to remember that religion was affecting city planning in Egypt.

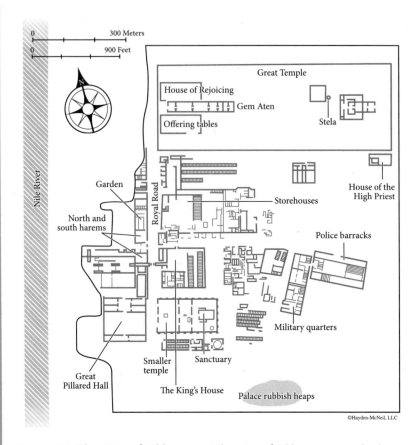

Figure 2.2 The City of Akhetaten: The city of Akhetaten was built as a royal capital for the pharaoh Akhenaten. The city fell equidistant between Memphis and Thebes and personified the new monotheistic cult of Aten.

Although the Egyptians' preponderance of the afterlife undoubtedly helped shape every urban center to some degree, trade also played an important role. Egypt was settled on a natural superhighway that allowed them, from earliest times, to enhance their urban makeup through trade. Egypt was an agrarian society throughout ancient history, becoming the "bread basket" of the world under the Romans. Certainly the development and the sustaining of fertile land played a major role in the evolution of all cities. Cultivated land normally fell directly on the east and west banks of the Nile, allowing the establishment of a necropolis and city further back. This worked well with the necropolis, because higher ground was always preferred for burial. Formal markets apparently were not a part of Egyptian cities until late antiquity. Vendors simply set up shop along streets under the shade of tree branches to sell whatever diversified goods that were available.

Internal trade must have been important, as it appears that the site of Alexandria was of some importance long before Alexander the Great conquered Egypt. That region, which the Egyptians called Rhacotis, was set up as a guard post to prevent the importation of foreign goods and the entry of merchants. When Alexander saw Rhacotis in 333 B.C.E., he probably viewed the area as important for two reasons. First, it offered a natural point to establish a permanent military station. Second, the ability to build an economic outpost to help connect his growing empire must also have been on his mind. Alexander, accompanied by a Greek architect named Deinocrates, personally went over the ground, marking out the site of the agora, the perimeter of the city walls, and location of the temples. Upon Alexander's death in 323 B.C.E., his empire would be split up among a few of his important generals. Ptolemy Soter gained the important area of Egypt, and his descendants would control the area until Cleopatra committed suicide in 30 B.C.E.

Unfortunately, Alexander never realized the impact that trade would have on this site. The Ptolemaic rulers certainly must have recognized the potential of its double harbor and position on the Mediterranean in becoming a major trading post in late antiquity (Figure 2.3). Strabo, writing in the beginning of the Roman period, comments on the city's commercial importance. He writes:

> "The advantages of the city's position are manifold, for; first, the site is washed by two seas, on the north by the so-called Egyptian Sea and on the south by Lake Mareia, or Marcotis. This is filled by many canals from the Nile, both from above (i.e. the south) and from the flanks, and the imports to the city by way of the canals greatly exceed those by the sea, so that the lake harbor was far richer than that on the sea; and here the exports from Alexandria also are larger than the imports...."

Alexandria, by the Ptolemaic period, had become the unrivaled center of world trade. It controlled imports and exports of Egypt and was also a great attractor for population. Native Egyptians, Jews, Syrians, Macedonians, and Italians were just part of the most populous city in the world by the late Ptolemaic period. If we are to believe observers of the day, the city could not have been smaller than 1,000,000 strong. One difficulty with studying Ptolemaic Alexandria is that it has been in use to the current day and subsequently built over several times. Although excavation has occurred on a limited basis, the leveling and reconstruction of the city from the Imperial Roman age forward leaves more questions than answers. We are aware of burial sites and wall formations, but street outlines are not as clear. History does tell us that a large Jewish population that filled both bureaucratic and trade positions lived in a specific neighborhood that was considered administratively separate, but other neighborhoods are not known to be as exact.

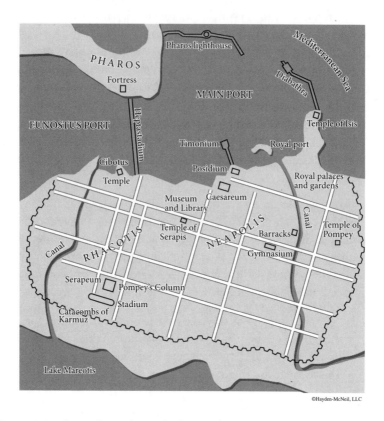

©Hayden-McNeil, LLC

Figure 2.3 Alexandria: The city of Alexandria was once an undeveloped area of land that the Egyptians called Rhacotis. Alexander the Great saw the potential of building a great market city that would dominate the Mediterranean Sea with two major ports.

When thinking of the evolution of the city during the Ptolemaic period, one must reference the growth of Alexandria. Canals were built to connect the Nile to Alexandria and harbors were developed to connect Egypt with the rest of the world. As well, its vast internal commerce leads us to believe that an industrial district existed. Its position and obvious marriage with trade both externally and internally developed the city into the greatest trade center of its time.

In 31 B.C.E., Anthony and Cleopatra's forces were defeated at the naval battle of Actium. The two fled back to Egypt, pursued by the victor Octavian, and took their own lives. Thus by 30 B.C.E., Ptolemaic rule had ceased to exist in Egypt and the era of Roman dominance began. Octavian, who later acquired the divine title Augustus, realized the importance of Egypt's agrarian output for the rest of Rome and put it more directly under his control than other provinces. Egyptian cities under Roman rule looked similar to Roman cities of the day, featuring a marketplace, temples, and avenues with monumental pillars, civic buildings, gymnasiums, and baths. The façade of the Roman Egyptian city remained similar from center to center. Originality was not a trait readily embraced by the empire. Behind the façade, Egyptian cities remained much as they were during the Ptolemaic period. Trade throughout the river valley remained the same, with the exception that taxation had changed slightly and the importance of the village had diminished, being eclipsed by more important trade centers.

If any aspect of Egyptian culture impacted the urban scene, it was the evolution of militarism. The degree in which militarism became an obvious part of cities and their planning became known throughout the ages. In the earliest predynastic period, walls may have been present around cities, but they soon became passé. The Narmer Palette, one of the most important artifacts of ancient Egypt, features a scene on the obverse side in which a bull is toppling a city wall and trampling a foe. The bull is interpreted as the pharaoh Narmer, who unified Upper and Lower Egypt, and ushered in the Old Kingdom. The palette infers that towns and cities surrounded themselves with walls at an early period when civil war took place (Figure 2.4). Lewis Mumford refers to Egyptian urban sites as "open cities" because much of their history was marked by the lack of walls. The reason walls are not found in Egypt during this early period is that Egypt itself was walled from outside intruders, with a marshy delta to the north and extraordinary deserts to the east and west. These geographic features were enough to give any prospective intruder pause. Those walls that existed during the predynastic age were torn down so as not to represent defiance against the pharaoh. Walls probably did not reenter the makeup of the city in Egypt until after the Hyksos' successful invasion (ca. 1,785 B.C.E.).

passé - outdated

Figure 2.4 The Narmer Palette: The obverse side of the Narmer Palette features a scene on the bottom station of a bull breaking through a fortification and trampling an individual. The bull is representative of Narmer, while the trampled individual represents vanquished opponents. The fortification supports the idea that walls played an important role in predynastic cities.

Knowing that she was no longer free from foreign attack, Egypt became very militaristic during the New Kingdom (1,558–1,058 B.C.E.). The pharaohs conquered vast territories to the south and east at this time, and the wealth of the empire mounted steadily. The success of Egyptian armies affected cities in a few different ways. First, victory always leads to tribute of some sort. For Egypt, this meant woods, ivory, copper, lead, precious stones, metals, and slaves. Cities like Thebes and Memphis received the lion's share of the tribute and used it toward improving city structures and building or improving temples (Figure 2.5). During the New Kingdom, cities like Thebes reached their pinnacle of greatness on the backs of subjugated people.

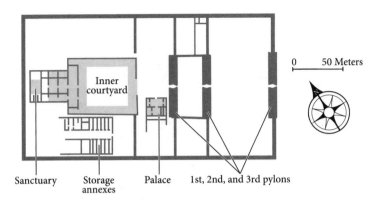

Sanctuary   Storage   Palace   1st, 2nd, and 3rd pylons
annexes

Figure 2.5 The Mortuary Temple of Ay: This temple, built for Ay, who succeeded Tutankhamun, exemplifies New Temple building. Ay built the inner temple and Horemb, his successor, built the outer temple. Horemb also removed Ay's name from the inner temple, thereby usurping the whole temple as his own.

As well, it is impossible to discuss the cities of Egypt in this period without elaborating on the importance of garrisons and citadels. Prior to the Hyksos' invasion, small standing armies defended both the north and the south in fortresses. Following the invasion and later expulsion of the Hyksos, the garrisoning of troops throughout Egypt became tantamount (Figure 2.6). As well, development of garrisons in cities throughout the growing empire became important. It is interesting to note that Egyptian texts of the New Kingdom period found in tombs include a single term that is translated as both city and fortress. One might infer that a military presence was so strong in some cities that drawing a difference between the two became difficult, if not impossible.

Certainly organic growth occurred in older nomes and cities like Thebes and Memphis, but simple geometric plans were also used in new towns. Often these simple geometric plans were meant for temporary living and offered an expedient way for a centrally located citadel to dominate an area. These geometrically planned cities were often work cities, but the New Kingdom pharaohs must have used this same mentality when overpowering enemies and establishing their dominance in foreign lands.

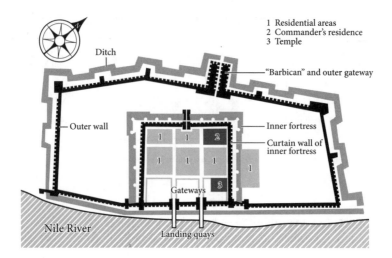

1 Residential areas
2 Commander's residence
3 Temple

Ditch

"Barbican" and outer gateway

Outer wall — Inner fortress

Curtain wall of
inner fortress

Gateways

Nile River — Landing quays

Figure 2.6 Buhen Fortress: The Nubian fortress was a large fortress situated in the south. The presence of this fortress first came into existence during the Old Kingdom. By the time of the New Kingdom it became more of a civilian settlement. Throughout Egyptian history, fortresses like these defended outposts from invaders.

As military dominance shifted from native control to the Greeks, then later to the Romans, city shape changed. Alexander the Great's entrance into Egypt in 331 B.C.E. had an immediate impact, as earlier noted, on the area called Rhacotis. There are varying reports of Alexander's entrance into this section of Egypt. But reports agree that it was Cleomenes of Naucratis and Deinocrates of Rhodes that helped Alexander lay out the city of Alexandria. The design of the city walls helped change what was a virtual frontier that was once influenced only by villages into a future megalopolis. But if we are to speak of militaristic influence of cities in Egypt, we must remember Aristotle. It is well known that Alexander's father, Philip of Macedon, hired Aristotle to be his son's tutor. Aristotle thought that the new trend among Greek towns to lay themselves out in a rectilinear fashion was ludicrous. He thought the design of cities was just one way in which defenses could be furthered. Rectilinear layout was fine in Aristotle's mind, but not for the entire city—it made invasion too simple. Although Ptolemaic Alexandrian streets are a bit sketchy, some general idea of the outline seems to agree with Aristotle's view.

Ptolemy Soter put a good deal of military emphasis on Alexandria and he made this, not Thebes or Memphis, his military base. Certainly a large military presence changed the shape of cities like Memphis to a certain extent, but nowhere in Egypt has a city been affected more by military than Alexandria. Thebes and Memphis would remain pharaonic in taste even with the traditional Hellenic buildings present. But it would be the hand of Alexander that would develop this outpost into what would become the greatest city of the Hellenistic Age.

Although Ptolemaic rulers impacted the cities of Egypt, it was not as uniform and mechanized as the Roman militaristic influence. Under the Ptolemies, Egypt was split into thirty administrative districts, or nomes, each governed by strategos. Augustus changed the power structure. He reduced the strategoi, who once had military and civil authority, to purely civil officials. Augustus maintained control of the land by stationing a legion in Alexandria, another near Memphis, and garrisons in key places. To defend all of Egypt, Rome made a commitment of approximately 20,000 men. The settlement of this many men meant the establishment of garrisons in Egypt throughout the land. No single garrison, with the exception of Alexandria and Memphis, maintained anything more than 1,000 to 1,500 men. Although this number may not have been more than .5 to .8% of the population, its impact on the city was still great. Outside of the standard Roman buildings, both small and large cities had army camps. These camps were sometimes inside the urban core and in a few instances, they were outside the urban center.

Cities like Hermopolis, Antinopolis, Oxyrhynchos, and Arsinoe were typical of smaller cities affected by Roman army presence. Not only did Roman armies change the shape of these Egyptian cities by adding the army camp, but they also added essential features to the centers that Romanized them. Roman temples, baths, agoras, theaters, streets, walls, and gates all became a new part of Egyptian city life under the Romans.

When considering the effect of philosophy on the evolution of Ancient Egyptian cities, one also notices changes that coincided with the philosophies that were introduced by different conquerors. Like early Ancient Mesopotamia, early Ancient Egypt philosophy was closely tied to religion and environment. We know already that the decline of interest in walls around cities stemmed from the fact that these people experienced so few invasions. Invasions were not a problem because the environment kept foreigners at bay, thus walls became unnecessary. In fact, the positive atmosphere led Egyptian people to view themselves as chosen people.

The religious symbolism that was apparent in the royal city of Akhetaten reflected some of the philosophy in building urban centers. Certainly one sees the obvious dualism that the Egyptians incorporated into buildings along the Nile. Important burials often occurred on the western side, where the sun set. Civic, administrative, and residential buildings would be to the east. The life-giving force of the sun was important in city building.

With the presence of Greek people as rulers in Egypt, so came a different philosophical view of cities. As previously mentioned, Aristotle must have had some influence on the layout of Alexandria, with disdain of a purely rectilinear layout a well-known fact. As well, Alexander was affected by other philosophers of the day that would later be known as Hellenistic. Alexander was heavily influenced by Diogenes the Cynic; in fact, Alexander once said if he had not been Alexander, he would have liked to be Diogenes. Diogenes' philosophical view of the city-state did not mesh with those of Aristotle. Aristotle felt the city-state was the highest form of organization man could enter. Diogenes, on the other hand, attacked the city-state as an institution. Alexander seemed to agree with Diogenes, as he spent his conquering years de-emphasizing the city-state. Early Stoics, Skeptics, and Epicureans agreed that man found happiness from within. The city recedes into the background as a place that develops the social consciousness of a people. Epicurean philosophy, which became popular in Alexandria, spoke about retreating from civic life. This disinterest in urbanity must have had some influence on Egypt in general during the Hellenistic period. The idea of the country being preeminent over the city definitely worked into the plans of a conqueror. It was easier to impose the will of the enfranchised over the newly subjugated people and place new emphasis on recent administrative centers like Alexandria.

Considering the positive notions that Hellenistic philosophy had on conquerors, it is not surprising that the Romans embraced their concepts. For a period, Epicureanism claimed the allegiance of some prominent Romans, including Calpurnius Piso and Cassius. Julius Caesar may also have been sympathetic to this school of philosophy. In the Roman world, Epicureanism seems to have been at its strongest before the fall of the Republic. But it did not suffer a sudden decline. Hellenistic philosophy worked so well with the Romans because their emphasis was on subjugation of people, and this philosophy encouraged and promoted the Romans to centralize lands and make cities less important. Part of this evidence is seen as Romans began reducing once-important cities to mere outposts and agrarian centers.

The history of planners in Egypt follows a more interesting course than that of Mesopotamia. The earliest record that historians possess regarding city planning dates back to the Twelfth dynasty at the worker's city of Kahun. As well, the city of Akhetaten also exemplifies a worker's city that was a bit more complex because it also served as a royal city during the reign of Akhenaten. Both cities are prime example of cities being built for religious reasons. The difference with Akhetaten is that a ruler helped plan the city and added to it a good deal of symbolism that drew off of his new monotheistic cult. Neither of these cities can be considered organic in growth, although we do see some organic growth outside of the central core section of the residential area for workers in Akhetaten. Memphis and Thebes were planned, but the planning took place earlier and probably with the goal in mind to control this lengthy ribbon of land that we call Egypt. Both were influenced by strongmen, men like Menes and Narmer in particular, and continued to grow in an organic manner. The best example of any planned city, though, is Alexandria. It is well known that Alexander himself laid out the city with the help of two professionals, Cleomenes and Deinocrates. There was no other city in Ancient Egypt planned with such determination. Perhaps this is the reason it was so successful. As far as Roman influence is concerned, we know that they superimposed their own order on the previous cities, adding military importance to some and removing greatness from others.

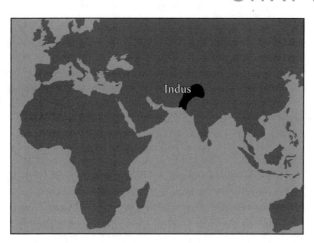

Indus

The origin of the Indus civilization is still debated among historians today. Many of the physical characteristics are similar to the Dravidian people who live in the Deccan Plateau of India today. Named after the great river system, on which many of its towns and cities were centered, the Indus civilization (ca. 2,500–1,750 B.C.E.) extended over a region larger than Egypt or Mesopotamia. Known also as the Harappan civilization or culture, after one of its most important sites, it covered a roughly triangular area of about half a million square miles. Most of the 150 known sites of the Bronze Age culture are in present-day Pakistan. The two largest sites, Mohenjo-daro in Sind and Harappa in Punjab, appear to have been the main centers.

The Indus civilization remained forgotten until the 1920s, when the first excavations were carried out at Mohenjo-daro and Harappa. In fact, the latter was first discovered in the 19th century, but its importance was not understood and it was heavily plundered when railroad construction was taking place. In 1931, another city was excavated at Chandu-daro, closer to the mouth of the Indus. Since then, further sites have been uncovered. Like its contemporaries in Mesopotamia and Egypt, the Indus civilization developed centers where trade, religion, militarism, and philosophy helped shape urbanization.

Our knowledge of the Indus civilization is not as great as that of the Mesopotamians and Egyptians. Virtually all their written literature was destroyed; the little that does exist is not deciphered well enough to give us a strong recorded testimony of their history. Due to this fact, one must rely on archaeological digs and material culture when making statements regarding the effect of religion on urbanization. This is not to suggest that religion did not play a role in the evolution and shape of the Indus city, because it is fair to say that religion was as important to the Indus city as it was to any civilization that preceded or succeeded it in antiquity.

There are certain general statements that can be made about the relationship between religion and society. Thus, a perceived relationship between religion and urbanity can be drawn. In the third and fourth millennium B.C.E., civilizations relied heavily on their god(s). Historians know that one of the popular cult figures in the Hindu pantheon today is Shiva, whose origin may have been founded in a fertility cult. A seal from the ancient city of Mohenjo-daro, part of the Indus civilization, already shows a figure that looks like an early Shiva. There is some historical evidence that Shiva is the oldest surviving cult in the world (Figure 3.1).

Figure 3.1 Shiva: Possibly the oldest surviving cult in the world is the Cult of Shiva. Evidence is found of this cult in the city of Mohenjo-daro.

One of the first characteristics of the Indus cities that strikes one when studying religious impact is that this civilization had no temples. The absence of temples does not mean that religion did not shape the urban form. It is true that there is no monumental religious architecture such as those found in Mesopotamia and Egypt, although at its height, the civilization had the ability to develop such structures. A study of the cities that were constructed articulates that the Indus people possessed more than adequate building and engineering skills. The reality is that building large temples was not important to their religion. Palaces are also not found in these Indus cities. This does not mean that the civilization was less advanced than any other urban structure. The Indus civilization simply found a more complex way to express their faith while living in a city structure.

There are many structures that can be found, particularly at Mohenjo-daro, that suggest religious structures. The most obvious structure is the Great Bath, elevated over the rest of the urban site. Not only is the Bath elevated but it is also secured from the lower town where residential features exist. Elevation and isolation within the city indicate that it was an area of great importance, and also helped develop the urban area. The obvious activity of the Great Bath is also important to the residents—here, members of society bathed and cleansed themselves in a ritual manner.

Scholars have argued that the Bath may have been a central complex for ritual bathing, linked to the religious life of the city. The Great Bath at Mohenjo-daro measured 180 by 108 feet. The central bathing area was 40 feet long and 23 feet wide and was made watertight by a layer of bitumen, filled with clay and faced with cut, burnt bricks. The bath's drainage system was sophisticated and included a specialized drain, more than six feet high, which ran underground and had a manhole cover that allowed it to be inspected. The main walls were more than six feet thick and their bricks were plastered with mud to reduce the effect of the salt in the bricks, which reacted with the heat and humidity of the area. Above the side rooms, some of which contained small baths, lay a flat roof made of planks and beaten earth resting on stout wooden poles. There is also evidence that a first story was added to the ground floor at a later date (Figure 3.2).

CHAPTER 3 Indus

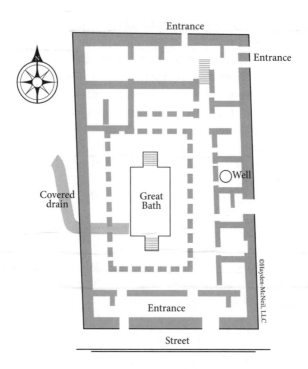

Figure 3.2 The Great Bath of Mohenjo-daro: The Great Bath of Mohenjo-daro was a central monument in this Harappan city that exemplified the importance of religion among this civilization.

It is tempting to speculate that the baths, partially because of their size, partially because of their location in the city, were of religious importance. Water has continued to be important to the dominant faith of India today. Modern Hindu temples have large holding tanks of holy water for purification. As well, the waters of the Ganges River are held sacred. Every devout Hindu wishes to cleanse their newborn in Ma Ganga and have their ashes spread there upon their death. In some areas, the water of the Ganges is believed to be so holy that it can purify the soul, releasing it from the cycle of rebirth once and for all. Water purification rituals continue to dominate many faiths (e.g., Islam and Christianity) and other ancient civilizations incorporated water into their religion. All of these facts lead to the conclusion that baths were tied to religion and were so important that they found themselves in an important location in the city.

Although temples did not dominate the urban scene as they did in Mesopotamia and Egypt, there is a possibility one existed in the citadel area of Mohenjo-daro or in the residential areas of other cities throughout the urban centers of the civilization. The fact that they were not prominent is important in and of itself. The people of the Indus, unlike Mesopotamians, Egyptians, Greeks, Romans, and Europeans, found the building of temples less important when shaping their cities. More significance was placed on shaping their cities in different ways. This is not to say that these people were less religious than other civilizations previously discussed; they simply chose to shape their cities in their own unique manner.

Other buildings existed near the Great Bath in Mohenjo-daro, which indicates that they were associated with religious activity. Across the street from the Great Bath sits the remnants of what must have been a noteworthy building. There is a good deal of disagreement as to the intention of this building, however. It is widely believed that this structure, often referred to as the College of Priests, had a significant association with the Great Bath. However, there is no strong evidence supporting its purpose, except that is was of meaningful size and was in a very important part of the urban site.

There are other buildings that have been identified as possible sites for religious buildings. In Mohenjo-daro there is a structure whose purpose was for something outside of a common domicile. This building, identified as House I in HR-A Area, was found with a large number of seals and sculptures inside. It also should be noted that it is three buildings interlinked into one another, and part of the construction is elevated and parallel to the Great Bath. There are other significant edifices built in various cities that might suggest religious association, but the purposes of those buildings are unclear. What is clear is that these were built in common areas, where ritual bathing took place, playing a role in developing its urban form.

Indus cities were planned in a regular pattern with a grid plan of straight streets, public wells, complete drainage, and citadels. The citadels, or fortresses, suggest a combined military and religious ruling power of the kind to be expected from all early civilizations. Unfortunately, the buildings do little to clarify a theocracy. However, the citadel that is set apart from the rest of the residences does not suggest a royal palace. In fact, no Indus city suggests that a royal palace existed.

The fact that royal palaces were not obvious may have a great deal to do with the environment of the region. Often the geography of a given civilization impacts why a city might form itself in a specific way. In many ways, ancient India was isolated from the rest of the world. Its geography provided its isolation. In spite of its size and diversity, until the oceans began to be opened up in the sixteenth and seventeenth centuries, India had to grapple with occasional, though often irresistible, incursions from distant explorers. To the north and northwest it was protected by some of the highest mountains in the world; to the east laid belts of jungle. The other two sides of the subcontinent's great triangle opened out into the huge expanses of the Indian Ocean.

Although long protected from external forces, India's northwestern frontier has been more open to the outside world than any other place. Baluchistan and the frontier passes were the most important zones of encounter between India and other peoples right up to the seventeenth century C.E.; in civilized times even India's contacts with China were first made by this roundabout route. At times, this northwestern region has fallen directly under foreign sway, which suggests that when we consider the first Indus civilizations, we do not know much about the way in which they arose, but we know that Mesopotamia and Egypt antedated them. Mesopotamian records indicate Sargon I of Akkad made contact with important trading partners that he called the "Meluhha." Current scholars believe that the Meluhha were the people of the Indus valley.

Like all early sites that would later evolve into cities, the early Indus civilization was purely an agrarian and pastoral economic system. Although we do not have a comprehensive indication of what the early culture grew, wheat and barley seemed to be a subsistence crop heavily relied upon. Different forms of millet were also planted during the peak of the civilization. The belief is that millet was first domesticated in southern central Asia and later found its way to southern Asia. As the northwestern frontier of Baluchistan seemed to stand out as an important area of encounter throughout its history, millet may have been passed to the civilization through paths in that region. Rice also became an important crop, but one must remember that so many varieties existed and so many in the subcontinent remained wild for so long that this corner of the world will have to wait for Chinese and other east Asian influence for a more domesticated crop.

Early sites in this Indus civilization also relied upon pastoralism for the early economy. The Indus relied more heavily on cattle and sheep than any other domesticated animals. In the early pre-urban years, this meant that the pastoral communities practiced a form of transhumance, a practice that saw them moving their herds to areas based on season and good grazing. The agro-pastoralist economy that existed in the pre-urban period did little in shaping the later cities that we marvel at today. Nothing more than temporary villages can be found as remains of these people, and certainly no complex form can be found.

As man became more sedentary, economics shaped the city dramatically. The Indus civilization possessed all the necessary prerequisites to be a high-functioning agricultural community: rich soil, proficient rainfall, and large rivers that could be manipulated through irrigation. But along with this was the reality of natural resources that were traded both internally and externally. Internal trade must have been high, based on the existence of a standardized system of weights and measures. That standardization also indicates strong communication throughout the land. Large public structures were built with thoroughfares that connected one important site to another. Markets were developed, both inside and outside the city walls. The external area was a large oval location that may have served as a standard market, or may have been used to tax traders before they entered the city. In the later historic era, caravans would stop outside of cities in the subcontinent at similar sites and would be processed by urban tax officials before they entered to ply their trade. Internally, markets were held in open courtyards and were far less formal, as the area was probably used for other public gatherings. Nevertheless, marketplaces were crucial to the Indus civilization that was developing niches in their economy. Their existence molded areas of the city.

In Mohenjo-daro, the most excavated city of this civilization, stands the remnant of a building that is currently called the Warehouse. It was made mostly of wood and sat near the Great Bath of the city. Scholars believe that the building stored items such as food, leather, fuel, wood, and cloth in finished and unfinished forms. The function of the Warehouse is unknown, but it does lead some to believe that a state-run economy may have existed. No other city had developed such a specialized area for bathing, although bathing was important throughout all of the civilization. This is evidenced through bathing areas in homes, but the Great Bath with the Warehouse must have been special. They were even separated at some distance from the rest of the urban area, placing significance on the ritualism that might have been taking place.

Another economic aspect that formed the city over time was the evolution of craftsmanship. Beyond the merchants, which were mentioned previously, textile workers, carpet makers, basket makers, and carpenters existed. Evidence in cities leads us to the conclusion that there were people that worked with bronze and copper. Independent professionals like doctors, builders, and architects found their homes in the city. These craftsmen would have needed a general site, such as a market, to ply their trade, but it is clear that the market was not a permanent site. There is a suggestion that some craftsmen used their homes as a base of work.

Beyond craftsmanship and the development of external and internal markets, the agrarian side of the economy led to the building of significant granaries. Like every successful civilization in the ancient world, surplus agriculture was a necessity. Farmers, who may have resided in Indus cities and went to the fields daily, raised grain that was then stored in elaborate structures. The granaries, as some of the dominant architectural features of the city, must have been a constant reminder to the urban residents of their reliance on agriculture for their success. The granary in Harappa is the most impressive building in the city, with walls that lay parallel to a central road. Storage and processing of the grain took place at this locale, which is known because ancient remains of husks have been found (Figure 3.3). Other cities in the civilization had granaries for their agrarian surplus, but none seem to be as significant as the granaries of Harappa.

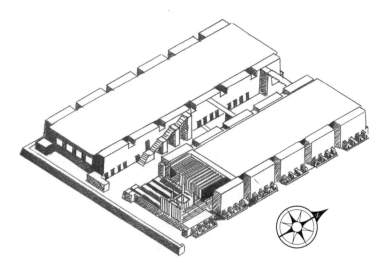

Figure 3.3 The Granary in the City of Harappa: In this artist's depiction of the granary at Harappa, the importance of agrarian surplus is apparent. Massive granaries were made in every city in the Indus civilization. This granary was so large that it could be seen from anywhere in the city. (Based on an illustration by Shelly Szuba.)

Before 2,000 B.C.E., the cities that had been established were trading far afield and living a life of some economic complexity. A great dockyard, connected by a mile-long canal to the sea at Lothal, four hundred miles south of Mohenjo-daro, suggests the importance of an external trade, which reached through the Persian Gulf as far north as Mesopotamia (Figure 3.4). In the Indus cities themselves, evidence survives of the specialized craftsmen drawing their materials from a wide area, and subsequently sending the product of their skills out again across its length and breadth. This civilization had cotton cloth (the first of which we have evidence) that was plentiful enough to wrap bales of goods for export whose cordage was marked with seals found at Lothal.

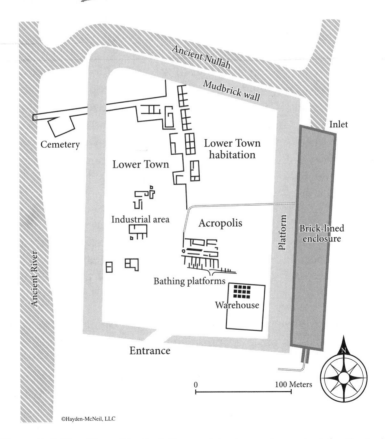

©Hayden-McNeil, LLC

Figure 3.4 The City of Lothal: External trade was important for the Indus civilization. In Lothal, a trade city was developed that had connections far afield. Goods that came to Lothal were disseminated throughout the civilization.

It is the seals that are found in sites like Lothal and others that confirm that the Indus civilization was a literate one. For a variety of reasons, extensive knowledge is not known of the language today. One reason is that when the Indus civilization fell in 1,500 B.C.E. to the Aryans, their conquerors were not literate themselves. This lack of literacy excluded a period of transition when multilingual documents were published. For all intents and purposes, no Rosetta Stone exists to decode the language of the Harappans. The seals that are left behind are beautiful stamps that linguists are attemping to decipher, so this civilization can be further understood.

Seals are found in many cities, but the center of Lothal has become a place where treasures of those stamps have been found. The location of seals demonstrates the full effect of trade on Lothal and the importance of external trade in other Indus cities. Lothal was a smaller center than Harappa and Mohenjo-daro, but it was an important trading town. Lothal, like other urban sites in this civilization, was rectilinear in outline. It was surrounded by an embankment and a level platform twelve feet in height, which formed the southeastern quarter of town and is believed to have served the same function as a citadel. Lothal was also a major industrial center, with craftsmen working copper, shell, and ivory. Kilns were present, so the center produced objects that were sent not only externally to other civilizations, but internally to other Indus cities.

A warehouse of significant size was found in Lothal not far from the docking area. This warehouse was the site of merchant activity and is the most important building in the city. It stresses that the city's main interest was trade. Its large canal also impresses upon us that the Indus civilization was not isolated from the rest of the world.

Past the clear impact that economics had on shaping the Indus city, military also had an obvious impact on its development. The dominating feature that relates to military in the Indus urban centers is the existence of citadels. A citadel is a fortress whose main goal is to protect a town or a city. It may be a part of the city or, in the case of the Indus civilization, stand separate. Some of the oldest known citadels in the world were found in the Indus civilization. The tallest citadel in the Indus Valley was over thirty-six feet tall. As A.E.J. Morris points out in *History of Urban Form*, each major city has an imposing citadel to the west of, and completely separate from, the main lower urban area.

These citadels are raised on high brick platforms and are surrounded by massive walls. Lower cities were similarly protected, but the citadel offered further protection from incursions and floods.

Morris gives a persuasive argument for why the citadel is outside the center itself, rather than within. Indus cities were rectilinear in layout, obviously planned. A citadel would have led to organic growth, something that was not favorable to the philosophy at hand. As well, a rectilinear layout may have been a military design. A layout of this type makes the movement of troops easier than many other layouts. The most important streets had a north/south orientation that were thirty feet wide, which would have allowed a large army to move freely in this direction. Contrary to this is the six to seven feet east/west orientation, which would have impeded movement of an organized force.

Geography may also have determined the location of the citadel. To a great degree the isolation of this people from the rest of the world led them to put less concern on the daily protection of their centers. Like the early Egyptians, the Indus civilization did not bother with walling their cities, because foreign incursion was not common. Ancient Mesopotamians were constantly fighting for control over their fertile soil, because they did not have an environment that dictated isolation like early Egypt and Harappa. Both Egypt and Harappa would later learn a hard lesson about not building walls when they were invaded and conquered. The building of the citadel in the Harappan city was also unnecessary, because the civilization did not appear to be one where a different class or groups of people were subjugating others, such as the case of the Romans in Europe. Citadels may have been more of a place to harbor people during floods than anything else.

The Indus civilization's view of philosophy is difficult to spend any expansive time discussing, because little literary evidence is left behind. Historians can only look at archaeological evidence to glean information of their philosophy and how it affected their development of the city. The first aspect of the city that strikes one is the obvious importance of cleanliness and how it became an important issue when shaping their city. As well, internal layouts of cities tell us that there was a strong concern for cleanliness and bathing; in some streets of Harappa, nearly every house has a bathroom. Even today, strong manifestations of bathing rituals in the Hindu religion still exist.

The lack of any single god dominating the city is also significant. Without a single god dominating the religious scene, there is no need to spend time building elaborate temples. The city is allowed to grow differently when there is no need to develop religious precincts like the Mesopotamians, Egyptians, Greeks, or Romans did. The clean rectilinear layout is possible when not interrupted by a series of temples and shrines. Out of all the civilizations studied, the Harappans have just as strong of a claim to make toward a city shaped by a philosophy. Unfortunately, unlike previous civilizations discussed, there is less fact to formulate theories.

If we can firmly comment on anything, it is the fact that Harappan cities were well planned. Morris argues, "They were the result of very early, if not the earliest, deliberate town planning processes." The rectilinear layouts of the cities are indicative that planners were involved in their development.

Both the Mohenjo-daro and Harappan centers had a number of similar features that support the idea that planners were involved. They were laid out on a regular grid of streets intersected by small lanes. Spiro Kostof notes, "A distinction was made between principal streets (as much as 20 to 30 feet—6 to 9 feet, wide) and the alleys onto which the houses looked." The sizes of the building blocks were identical, with baked bricks being used; also, there were highly organized drainage systems.

Nothing illustrates the existence of planning more than the drainage system that was in every city in the Indus civilization. Every civilization must deal with the eventuality of handling waste. Some think about it less than others. Elizabethan England modeled an open sewage plan where waste was tossed onto the street. Pigs were also employed to deal with the city's sewage. Moving about England could be delicate at times, and crossing a street was downright treacherous. But long before England, the Indus civilization spent a good deal of time planning a complicated system that dealt with all of their waste and bath water.

One-third of all houses had their own well to use. Additionally, multiple wells were found throughout the cities that were communal in nature. In Mohenjo-daro, seven hundred wells were found in total. Some cities, like Harappa, used the Indus River to draw fresh water. Still other cities diverted river water and caught rain in reservoirs to use. Some cities had multiple sources of water. The most impressive room in a house in an Indus city was the bathroom. Baths existed in homes; even showers, in some of the more advanced bathrooms. The bathroom was smooth with a slope that led to a small drain that existed in one corner of the room. The water would empty into a very efficient drainage system that exemplifies the important engineering skills and planning that existed.

Private bathrooms were found in almost every house in the city. Most offered a jar that was lowered into the floor and connected to the drainage system. In rare cases, the hole had a seat one could rest on. Waste water would find itself flowing into the street and was covered with brick. The drain could be inspected at intervals through ancient manhole covers. All of this waste was discharged outside of the city. Much thought had to go into the planning of the cities and these special ways of handling waste and water (Figure 3.5).

Figure 3.5 Culvert: This image of a culvert illustrates the organized way waste was handled in Indus cities. Using standardized burnt bricks, Harappans built culverts throughout the city that carried waste below the street level and deposited it outside of the urban site.

Other evidence of planning can be found near the citadel. There were a number of important buildings in the citadel. The names used for these structures were given to them by the excavators and were suggested by their appearance and possible function. On the west lay the granary, the remains of which consists of solid blocks of brickwork divided by passages. This surviving podium originally supported a timber superstructure, and the layout of the passages between the blocks meant that air could circulate beneath the building. There is disagreement over whether grain that was stored here was state grain, accumulated through taxes, or whether it was kept there for times of famine. Nevertheless, a conscious effort was made to make this a part of the city (Figure 3.6).

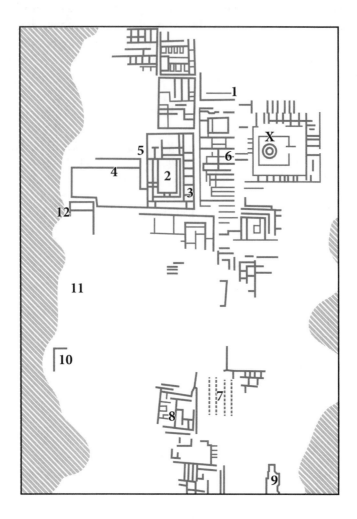

Figure 3.6 The Citadel Area of Mohenjo-daro: The citadel area in every Indus city had several important buildings congregated around them. The following letter and numbers represent what scholars believe took place in the given area.

X – The citadel—Later a Buddhist stupa was built on its remains
1 – College
2 – Great Bath
3 – Guest rooms
4 – Granary
5 – Drain attached to Bath
6 – Residence for priests

7 – Assembly hall
8 – Temple complex
9 – Bastions
10 – Tower
11 – Mud-brick embankment
12 – Stairs

East of the granary was the Great Bath, possibly used for ritual bathing. But the purpose of the two other buildings on the citadel—the so-called college and assembly hall—is not known. In the lower town, several of the houses were spacious, with bathrooms, toilets, proper drainage, water supplies from their own wells, and hearths for fires. The larger ones were built around a courtyard and had stairs up to a flat roof. The less wealthy lived in cramped conditions in houses with one or two rooms. Most buildings were made of baked brick, and the streets had drains covered in brick, with holes for inspection. Also in this part of town were the workshops for the many craftsmen of the city.

Although the Greeks have been credited in the past with the earliest form of town planning, one only needs to look at the layout of Mohenjo-daro or Harappa to realize that these gridiron plans predate the Greeks. Unfortunately, our lack of literary sources from this period makes it impossible to credit planners more specifically.

CHAPTER 4

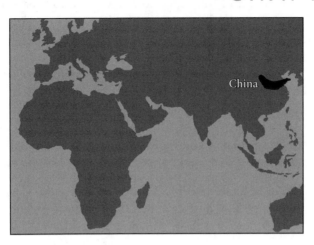

China

China

China has been the most populous nation on the Earth for the last two thousand years. Throughout history, it has comprised approximately one-quarter of mankind and has continued to dominate this demographic category. Although India may surpass China in the future, this long history of population was one of the many reasons that urbanization took root in the area. Although it is generally accepted by historians that the sedentary cultures that led to urbanization could first be found in the Middle East around the fourth millennium B.C.E., within 2,000 years, urbanization would have spread throughout all of Eurasia.

The emergence of the Chinese urban culture at the most eastern end of Asia during these 2,000 years seems to have had no direct connection with the urbanization of the west. The disagreement over whether China was influenced by other civilizations is still unsettled by scholars, but there is a considerable amount of evidence that supports the Chinese were more isolated than any other old world civilization. The major support behind this isolation argument is the geography that surrounded the earliest culture. Geographically, the plains area where early cultures evolved was surrounded by deserts (Gobi and Taklamakan), mountain ranges (Himalaya, Karst, Huang Shan, and Zhang Jia Jie), and the Tibetan Plateau in the western regions that would have mightily impeded travel to the east. Coupled with this was an expansive coast that found no visitors from the west approaching. Geography left the Chinese isolated and developing urban centers under only their domain.

The earliest development of this region that gives rise to urban concepts took place during the Neolithic Age, when man transitioned from being nomadic to sedentary. The earliest archaeological site that supports sedentary living in China can be found at Banpo. Banpo was located in the Yellow River Valley and gives several examples of organized Neolithic settlements that began circa 4,700–3,600 B.C.E. The area of this settlement is 500–600 acres and is surrounded by a ditch, probably meant as a defensive moat, fifteen to eighteen feet wide. The houses at Banpo were circular and semi-subterranean. There appears to have been communal burials and pottery kilns outside of the moat.

Neolithic urbanization begins with the Yang Shao culture, of which the Banpo settlement is the best example. Banpo was found in the central plain called Zhogyuan, near the lower reaches of the Yellow River. This area is often referred to as the cradle of Chinese civilization. Here Banpo grew from a typical Yang Shao village in both size and organization until the construction of the Great Hall ca. 4,000 B.C.E. Like Eridu in Mesopotamia, Banpo in east Asia was the first instance of specialized architecture, something other than a house. The Great Hall became the prototype of later palaces and imperial cities.

Physically, Banpo was composed of 200 round pit houses and the Great Hall across five hundred acres, surrounded by a ditch. These pit houses were built for solar gain, as the doors were directed so maximum sunlight could be gained. Already, even at this early stage, the principle of south-facing entrances was firmly established. The needs and beliefs of Banpo society created the prototypical Chinese urban form. In the springtime, sacred procreation sites became the Holy Place. Moreover, the connection between ancestors, earth, and fertility developed into the theories of qi and feng shui. Qi, according to ancient Chinese philosophy, is the vital energy believed to circulate the body in currents, while feng shui is a Chinese system believed to use the laws of both Heaven and Earth to help one improve life by receiving positive qi.

The *Book of Burial* elaborates this theory. Man is considered concentrated qi, when his bones are returned to the earth they become re-energized by qi. The living descendants are affected by the qi generated from the bones of their ancestors, "as a lute string will pick of the vibration of another lute string near it." In this theory, the world was an active matrix of qi into which graves, houses, and cities must be carefully inserted by feng shui principles to maintain harmony. The shape of this world was described by a parallel cosmology of a round heaven revolving around a square earth. Cosmology is the branch of philosophy dealing with the origin and general structure of the universe.

Cosmology was often exemplified through artwork. There are many examples carved in jade of the bi and the cong. The bi, a circular object, represents the heavens, while cong, a square-like object, represents the earth. This cosmology originated from Neolithic astronomy. There are examples of Yang Shao pottery decorated with the Big Dipper inscribed on a nine-in-one square (Earth) surrounded by a circle (Heaven), which depicts a cosmic diagram of Earth divided into nine parts. This nine-in-one square, in time, became the basis of the well-field system, which was the basic geometric and legal module of urban-regional planning. The well-field system was a Chinese land distribution system that finds its origins in the Neolithic Age and lasted until the end of the Period of the Warring States. Its name comes from the Chinese character 井 (jǐng) which means "well" and looks somewhat like the # symbol (Figure 4.1). The symbol represents the theoretical appearance of land division. A square area of land was split into nine identically sized sections; the eight outer sections were privately cultivated by serfs and the center was communally cultivated on behalf of the landowning aristocrat. While all fields were aristocrat-owned, the private fields were managed exclusively by serfs and the produce was entirely the farmers'. It was only produce from the communal fields, worked on by all eight families, that went to the aristocrats, and which, in turn, could go to the king as tribute.

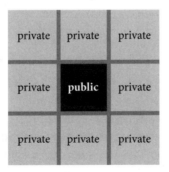

Figure 4.1 The Well-Field System: This system represents the Chinese land distribution that dates back to the Neolithic Age. Notice the land in the center that was publicly cultivated went exclusively to the aristocrat. Private land was managed by serfs and the produce ended up in their hands.

This early system of land distribution is undoubtedly tied to early religious beliefs. As will be seen as the history of urban development in ancient China is discussed, religion played a dominant role in shaping the urban form. Before the whole of China united under the rule of the First Emperor during the Third century B.C.E., the nonagricultural settlements had developed into real towns and cities. Many of them were of considerable size in area as well as in population; some of them had even grown into multifunctional regional centers.

It can be argued that prior to the Zhou dynasty, cities were simply ritual centers. Surrounding these areas were workshops and artisan settlements where ritual implements, weapons, and the adornments of the rulers were made. From the Zhou dynasty forward, these ritual centers became large urban settlements of several square miles, surrounded by a wall of compacted earth. The planning and construction of such a city became a ritual act in itself, and the layout of the city followed sanctified formal rules.

When religion or theocracy ruled the day, as it did for some time with the Chinese, rulers went to great extents to articulate their tie to religion. This often meant building temples not far from the seat of power. Axial alignment was most commonly used in association with an overall urban diagram. Planners had to consider three factors: cosmology, physical geography, and cultural geography.

Chinese city planners emphasized the north–south axis to order cities. This north–south axis developed the image of a meridian and gave order to their space. This axial design was closely tied with the concept of the universe and the place of the ruler in it. The ancient Chinese name "Zhongguo" for China is translated as "The Middle Kingdom." This concept of centrality can be found in the development of their cities. The Chinese believed that the Earth was a stable cube in the universe; the heavens were round. The space was conceived as tiles overlapping one another and at the center lay the capital of the empire, oriented to the points of the compass. In the center of the capital sat the imperial palace that commanded a north–south axis within the city. All important buildings were on a north–south axis. Buildings faced south in the direction of the Red Phoenix, of summer and fire. From the north came the winter and destructive hordes. Its color was black, and the emperor never faced it unless he addressed gods or ancestors.

In Chinese cities, everything about the urban form was affected by religious function. Even houses were standardized by an official code that dictated size and placement in the city. The palace of the Emperor was oriented to the seasons and heavens. The celestial plan, called the Great Plan, was given, according to myth, to the first dynastic emperor by the deity that invented surveying. The plan was ninefold and the center of the universe was found in the palace. This meant that anytime the palace moved, so did the center of the universe.

Capital cities were laid out in two basic ways. Both models were so ancient that they existed before the birth of Jesus. By the time the Roman Empire had reached its period of rule under Augustus in the First century C.E., there was a great deal of discussion regarding city planning in China. First, the square or rectangular urban form was in place. The palace in this design was placed on the northern end of the city, facing south. Cities were aligned in the four cardinal directions. Each direction had significance that could be tied to the religious beliefs. Urban cults forced the development of cities in this way. Each direction represented a functional zone such as the area of imperial ancestors, the god of soil, and Heaven. These formalized plans were much more difficult in the south near the Yangtze River, where land is more mountainous (Figure 4.2).

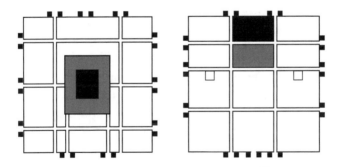

Figure 4.2 Capital City Models: The two models used in ancient Chinese imperial capitals are represented above. Either the city had a palace in the center of the city, as in Beijing, or the palace was centered into the back of the city wall, as in Chang'an. All palaces had entrances facing the south.

In the second capital scheme, the palace was in the center of the city. This example can be seen in Beijing. Beijing, formerly the capital of Dadu, seat of Kublai Khan's empire, revived this plan from an earlier period. The Beijing model finds its foundation in a First century C.E. religious book entitled *Zhou Li* (Rituals of [king] Zhou). The text states that, "It is the sovereign alone who establishes the states of the empire, gives to the four quarters their proper positions, gives to the capital its form and to the fields their proper divisions. He creates the offices and apportions their functions, in order to form a center to which the people may look." The foundation of early and even late ancient Chinese cities always reflects the effect of religion in its planning and form.

The development of many ancient cities in China was affected by much more than religion, though. The development of trade also played a major role in urban evolution among the Chinese. Chang'an was the most renowned city of ancient China and exhibits the effect of commercialism on city form. Chang'an was the capital of both the Han and the Tang dynasties, reaching its peak of development under the Tang in the Eighth century C.E., when it contained a population of two million people. The central northern division contained the palace, as well as the palace city with the main court offices and altars for the ritual ceremonies that the emperor performed. East and west of the palace city were two sections with large building lots; south of those were two more sections with the normal residential areas, each containing a large market on the main east–west thoroughfare. The central south section contained the largest streets that ran through the city from north to south for about three miles. All sections were subdivided into 108 wards that were walled. The wards were established early in the city's history.

The walls that surrounded the wards had two to four gates, which were closed at night. No buildings, but only walls, were on the roads, and they were patrolled by police. The two big markets were also surrounded by walls, and business transactions were watched by a special market police force. The markets were also closed at night. Emperors found it necessary to create such strict controls on the markets because China was a very diverse place, and people were often deported to the Chinese capital so a more watchful eye could be placed on malcontents.

This diversity could also be seen in the development of trade associations. Cities had urban guilds that coexisted with associations that were tied to localities outside of the urban site. Certain crafts were related to different parts of the empire. The locality and their craft were represented in the city, so carpenters or textile merchants would hail from an area outside of the city and compete for space in major cities like Beijing. These non-citizens were treated differently and lived in different areas. Even their bodies, upon death, were stored in a special mortuary to be returned to their homeland.

Smaller cities were affected by markets in a much more dramatic way. As larger cities had a tendency to be planned, smaller cities experienced a more organic growth that transcended the development one would find in Chang'an. Much earlier sites, like Zhengzhou, a Shang capital in northern China, were made up of residential communities that were built very close to one another. Cities like Zhengzhou were unique in that there were no centralized institutions that predicated its development. In fact, no monument building is found at this site. Rather, this urban structure existed because of the groups of farmers, tradesmen, fishermen, and elites who existed there that provided services and goods to the frontier. The development of a city of this sort supports the argument that the city comes into existence when it is large enough to be self-sufficient. This self-sufficiency came from the interactive trade that residents offered one another.

There was a breakdown in the political organization and structural decline within the heartland of China during the second half of the Tang dynasty. One important change that takes place is that the imperial government moved from the heartland further east and north. The old imperial centers were never used again, and therefore, trade changed. Coupled with this move was the migration south of the majority of people. This caused an economic revolution that changed the urban site.

Prior to this period, large masses of people had gravitated around capitals and garrison towns in the north to create a significant consumer population. To support these masses, agrarian surplus was transported north from the Yellow River Valley via the Grand Canal that was built to connect the Yellow and Yangtze Rivers. This Grand Canal, which is still in use today, connected consumer areas in the north with the production areas in the southeast. Increasing demands nurtured more production of staple food and consumer goods.

As the population shifted south during the second half of the Tang, it took on the character of colonization. Many families leaving the north looked for opportunities to become rich and powerful. These families found themselves making a living in commerce. This desire was facilitated by the evolution of a market economy in the rural areas. Here in the south, in the second half of the Tang, was primitive self-sufficiency coupled with a new market economy filled with goods and ideas.

CHAPTER 4 China

Despite the decline that was experienced by the empire at this time, economic activities increased considerably. Less governmental control led to more success in the free-market economy throughout the entire empire. In association with this virtual revolution in the economic market was an agricultural market that was growing due to advances. Agricultural production reached an all-time high for the Chinese in the ancient period.

This period of political fragmentation can be compared to the fragmentation that was experienced during The Period of the Warring States that ended in 221 B.C.E. These periods are also comparable in that both were followed by eras of splendor so renowned that the westerner Marco Polo wrote of them after his odyssey to the east that kept him at the court of the Great Khan some nineteen years. Polo was not alone in his discussion of China's grandeur; any merchant traveling along the Silk Road spoke of its greatness.

The impacts on urban development were many, but a few can be outlined as important in changing the structure of the urban site. First, along with the weakening of the political system, was the diminished control on the market system and wards. At this point people were able to select where they could live and how they would conduct business in the city. When the Song established their dynasty in the Tenth century C.E. and established the capital in Kaifeng, the city was only remodeled; no new planned capital was built. This resulted in a mixed and complex land use pattern; the main feature was the development of market streets within the residential areas. Only the palace complex was separated and hidden behind walls.

The second aspect was the development of commercial suburbs outside the city walls, sometimes surrounded by a second earthen wall that was in many cases larger than the original city. These suburbs contained the newly developed market streets along the main traffic routes or along the canals in the southern cities. In Dadu, the capital of the Yuan dynasty and today's Beijing, Marco Polo tells us, "Outside of each gate is a suburb so wide that it reaches to and unites with those of the other nearest gates on both sides, so that the number of inhabitants in these suburbs exceeds that of the city itself." Separate accounts support Polo's claim that the city of Hangzhou's inner city contained 400,000, while the suburb rose to 600,000 by the early Thirteenth century C.E. This population explosion occurred due to vast interest in trade in China.

The third aspect is the development of rural market towns between administrative centers. This started in the early Tang in the Seventh century C.E., but gained momentum in the Ninth century and in the Fourteenth century, when the rural market towns were more than four times the number of the administrative centers. Of the 6,000 or so urban places, about 1,400 were administrative centers—of which 500 may have had a population of more than 4,000 inhabitants and contained about half the total urban population; that is, about 5% of the total population of the empire. This furthers the discussion of economics and trade-shaping cities in China. It should be noted, though, that when strong central control disappeared, economics shaped other smaller urban sites throughout the realm.

As has been noted in previous chapters, religion and economics have played significant roles in shaping the urban form, but militarism was also significant in the city's development. Each dynasty in China came to power after a military struggle took place. As well, the Period of the Warring States, which was an internal struggle that lasted over 200 years, clearly ingrained upon the Chinese people the importance of the defense of their important cities. This need to defend cities and populations influenced the urban shape.

City walls have long been pointed to as an important factor in the development of the shape of the city. Nothing exemplifies the Chinese response to militarism in the city more than their prolific wall building. During the earliest dynasty, the importance of the wall is articulated in their ideograph for the word city. The Shang ideograph for "city," during this dynasty was a kneeling individual beneath a city wall. Although the wall signifies the importance of the military defense that the Shang offered its citizens, it also demonstrates the submission to the state and the burden of citizenship (Figure 4.3). The Chinese word for wall, in a narrow sense, specifically refers to defensive walls built around a city or town. In classical Chinese, the word means the defensive wall of the "inner city," housing government buildings. There are separate Chinese words that mean the defensive wall of the "outer city," protecting mainly residences. The phrase "the Long Wall" specifically referred to the Great Wall.

Figure 4.3 "City:" The Shang ideograph for city is a kneeling individual underneath a city wall. This articulates the importance of early wall construction. (Based on an illustration by Shelly Szuba.)

Like various other innovations in Chinese history, the invention of the city wall is attributed to a semi-mythological sage; in this case, to Xia dynasty (ca. 2,070 B.C.E.–ca. 1,600 B.C.E.) leader Gun, the father of Yu the Great. It is said that Gun built the inner wall to defend the prince, and the outer wall to settle the people. An alternative theory attributes the first city wall to the Yellow Emperor, a historic ruler during the latter part of the Period of the Warring States. A number of Neolithic-period walls surrounding substantial settlements have been excavated in recent years. These include a supposed wall at a Liangzhu culture site, a Neolithic culture that developed in the Yangtze River Delta region ca. 3,400 B.C.E.–ca. 2,200 B.C.E., a trapezoidal stone wall at Sanxingdui that sits on the Yazi River, a Bronze and Neolithic culture founded ca. 1,600 B.C.E., and several tamped earth walls at the Longshan culture site in the late Neolithic that settled near the Yellow River Valley ca. 3,000 B.C.E.–ca. 2,000 B.C.E. These walls generally protected settlements the size of a large village and demonstrate that the concept of wall building was widespread.

In Shang dynasty China, large walls were erected in the Fifteenth century B.C.E. that had dimensions of 65 feet in width at the base and enclosed an area of some 2,100 yards squared. In similar dimensions, the ancient capital of the State of Zhao, which was one of the seven major states during the Period of the Warring States, founded in 386 B.C.E., had walls that were also 65 feet wide at the base, a height of 50 feet tall, with two separate sides of its rectangular enclosure measured at a length of 1,530 yards.

Most towns of a significant size possessed a city wall from the Zhou dynasty onward. For example, the city wall of Pingyao was first constructed between 827 B.C.E. and 782 B.C.E. Prior to their demolition in the 1960s and 1970s, the city wall of Suzhou largely followed the same plan as set down by Wu Zixu—a famous militarist during the Spring and Summer Period, which preceded the Period of the Warring States in the Fifth century B.C.E. By the Yuan dynasty, it was government policy that towns that were administrative seats of county-level units or above were to have defensive walls. In ancient China, sieges of city walls were portrayed on bronze vessels dating back to the Period of the Warring States. This demonstrates how important walls were to the evolving empire and intimated that their existence would continue to play an important role in urban form.

This aspect of defense went a long way toward determining where markets arose in the urban sites. As mentioned earlier, wards and markets were walled off, less to defend against foreign incursion than to control their own citizens. Once decentralization occurred in the empire, markets and wards were less controlled and walls were meant for protection of important capitals and regional cities. Walls were built to help emphasize the power of the sitting ruler and the influence he could exert over his lands.

Although militarism played a significant role in shaping aspects of the city, Chinese philosophy would be crucial in virtually every aspect of its form. From the earliest period, China has presumed that their role was central in the development of humanity. This thought process is yet another reason that the Chinese found it fitting to call their realm the Middle Kingdom. This philosophical view that they were in the center of the world gave them a concentric worldview that influenced urban form. Early Chinese writing embraced the idea of a concentric view that consisted of five concentric zones with a royal capital in the center.

In this concentric model, the first zone of 500 Li (approximately 150 miles) is occupied by the royal domains, while the second zone, also 500 Li, is the zone of the princes. The third zone, 500 Li, was considered the zone of pacification, while the fourth zone is settled by "half civilized barbarians." The final zone, the fifth, is where the "cultureless barbarians" lived. The total area covered in this concept is roughly comparable to today's Inner China, the ancient China of the 18 provinces (Figure 4.4).

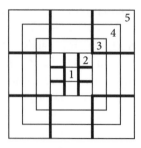

Figure 4.4 The Concentric Model of the Middle Kingdom: The Chinese perceived their entire world in a concentric model, with the royalty occupying the center. This conceptually covered the entire modern Inner China. (Based on an illustration by Shelly Szuba.)

Not surprisingly, the philosophical underpinnings that described how China itself was organized transcended to the city. Chinese philosophy is closely tied to religion, so some thoughts seem repetitive in nature, but there are enough different influences derived from philosophy worth mentioning. The use of Confucian rites to guide urban planning could be traced back to the *Rites of Zhou*, a book written in the late Spring and Autumn Period. The Spring and Autumn Period took place after the years of the fall of Zhou and before the Period of the Warring States, approximately 722–483 B.C.E. During this period, a series of philosophical thoughts arose, the most significant of which would be Confucian thought, Daoism, and Legalism. The "State Management System" in *Rites of Zhou* had a profound influence on the urban planning; in particular, capital planning in Chinese history. It put forward the ideal urban planning model and sketched the basic contour of city planning in ancient China. Meanwhile, in the "State Management System," some ritual thoughts like "choosing the center to build," "holding the center as superior," are also reflected in urban planning.

One philosophical notion that was imbedded in Confucian thought as well as many other Chinese philosophies was the idea of yin and yang. Yin and yang are the philosophies used to describe how opposite or contrary forces are interconnected and interdependent in the natural world. This concept could be applied to anything in the natural world, and cities were no exception.

Yin and yang philosophical concepts were used in Chinese city planning in early dynastic rule, but were not widespread until the Zhou. The initial concept of planning a city in China was based on the idea of an enlarged Holy Field. The Holy Field symbol is essentially numerology applied to the nine-in-one square. Each square is numbered 1–9 to form a magic square. This symbolism had existed since the Xia dynasty; however, this symbolism became fully expanded to numerology during the Zhou dynasty. The Holy Field was used to conceptualize many systems, such as astronomy, geography, and politics. The center is the subject of the system, the inner eight squares represent the means through which the subject acts, and the twelve outer edges are amplifications of their qualities. The four squares of even integers at the corners are yin, and the five axial squares of odd integers are yang. This was considered the correct balance of yin and yang to keep a harmonious qi or vital energy (Figure 4.5). The ideal city was therefore a diagram of this multipurpose heavenly symbol drawn upon the landscape. The *Rites of Zhou* codified how the Holy Field would be transformed into a city. Moreover, it dictated planning from a residential to regional scale.

4	9	2
3	5	7
8	1	6

Figure 4.5 The Holy Field: The Holy Field embraced the philosophical concept of yin and yang. In order to keep a harmonious qi, a correct balance of odd and even integers had to be met. The ideal city followed this diagram when planning. (Based on an illustration by Shelly Szuba.)

The construction of the capital city by the artisans was standardized. Each side is approximately two miles in length with three gates, nine longitudinal and nine latitudinal lines divide the interior of the city with north to south roads, nine times a carriage gauge in width, the ancestral temple is on the left (of the palace city in the middle), and altars for the god of land and the god of grains are on the right side. The palace faces the imperial court and is backed against the market.

A temple of ancestors was placed in square 7, a temple of agriculture in square 3, and an audience hall in square 1. The market was not considered of high importance and was placed in square 9 to the north of the palace. The palace was located in square 5 of the Holy Field, which was enclosed by fortifications to form the Inner City. The edge of the Holy Field was enclosed in a second ring of fortifications and referred to as the Outer City. The fortifications were specified as 60 feet wide and 45 feet high. The wall of the Outer City was pierced by 12 gates aligned with three major north–south avenues and three major east–west avenues. Parallel with these avenues were six minor avenues for a total of nine avenues running north–south and nine avenues running east–west. These 18 avenues were specified as the width of nine chariots (90 feet) and divided the city into the wards, which were discussed earlier.

Conceptually, each ward was an individual village; thus the capital consisted of 81 villages within a wall. Inside each ward, individual land was parceled out in modules. Each module could accommodate one aristocratic residence or be subdivided into as many as six smaller residential plots. The flexibility of this simple system allowed great diversity within each ward, but great homogeneity at the city scale.

The Zhou classical standard extended the concept of modular planning used in the Capital to the regional planning scale. The city was part of a modular regional system of urban economics. It mirrored the hierarchy of the state at a smaller scale. Each module in the hierarchy, whether urban or rural, therefore had the same population base and political power. The economic rank of a city determined its size, which was set by the emperor.

The grid plan that was apparent in ancient Chinese cities is a statement of the involvement of planners as well. The grid pattern that has been applied throughout the world is normally a statement that articulates an authoritative government. In the first centuries of imperial Chinese history, the administrative capital was an act of total creation. The city was entirely planned, with nothing organic taking place. The fact that philosophical, religious, militarism, or economic driving forces existed is true, but it was the authoritarian nature that overrode the planning. This form of planning is often referred to as orthogonal planning. Orthogonal planning reflects that there is an unalterable hierarchy. It enveloped the palace with different classes and minimized the role of the market, which was considered less important until the Tenth century C.E.

Few urban planners are known of in ancient China, but later cities like Chang'an and Dadu, today's Beijing, are known. Yuwen Kai and Liu Bingzhong are probably the best-known planners of the era. Both planners worked later in the imperial history, with Yuwen Kai designing Chang'an during the Sui dynasty and Liu Bingzhong planning the construction of Dadu during the Yuan dynasty.

Yuwen Kai was born into a noble family that established themselves in the field of militarism. Yuwen Kai had been a long-term official of the Sui dynasty, in charge of a variety of major construction projects. Before taking on the role of urban planner of Chang'an, we know that Kai had supervised the construction of many large scale architectures and other major cities. Quite a few huge civil engineering projects built during the Sui dynasty, such as Daxing City, East Capital Luoyang, the Guangtong Canal, restored Old Luban Road, and the Great Wall, were completed under his planning, design, and leadership.

Liu Bangzhong can, in many ways, be called the founder of modern Beijing. He not only set up a series of political systems for the Yuan Empire, but also planned the construction of Dadu. Dadu became the capital built closest to the rules of *Rites of Zhou* among all the capitals of China. The design of the Yuan dynasty's capital Dadu was dominated by the capital building thoughts of Han Chinese rulers; namely, the system of imperial court in the front, marketplace at the back, and ancestral temple on the left.

In short, planning was dominated by the power of those who ruled and was influenced by the major concepts put forward. Religion and philosophy influenced the layout and cardinal direction of the city, as well as markets that were less influential when the emperor was more dominant and more influential when the emperor was less dominant. Militarism was perhaps less of a driving force than it was in other civilizations due to the isolation that the Chinese geography offered.

●CHAPTER 5

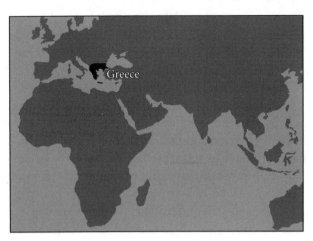

Greece

The river valley civilizations had commonality concerning their geography. As well, similarities were also apparent in the way in which religion shaped their early cities. In Mesopotamia, agrarianists of the Tigris and Euphrates River Valley gravitated toward worship centers where cities eventually crystallized. In Egypt, religious centers gave rise to worker cities or, in rare occasions, a temporary royal city. The Indus civilization deemphasized religious centers, while purification rituals influenced urban form. In China, early religious beliefs laid the foundation for most cities. As the focus shifted toward the Aegean and into the Greek world, religion continued to exert influence on the development of cities, but its influence in the Hellenic civilization is not nearly as significant as the civilizations previously mentioned.

It is impossible to think of the Greeks without conjuring up images of their immense pantheon. In a prescientific society, their rich mythology was necessary to help explain the complex world that surrounded them. All Greek cities had at least one thing in common: their dependence on the gods. They provided a continuity of power which at times seemed to use their human counterparts as mere playthings. One only needs to peruse Homer's *Iliad* or *Odyssey* to grasp how entwined these gods were in mortal lives. No city could exist without the gods; their contribution to the urban area was almost continuous. It was not until the Seventh or the Sixth century B.C.E. in Greece that the idea developed of providing the gods with monumental buildings transpired.

The fact that religion expressed less of an influence on classical Greek cities than previous ancient cities might date back to the Minoan culture that developed on Crete and heavily affected the later Hellenics. The island of Crete was an important island situated in the Mediterranean Sea. Three Late Bronze Age (ca. 1,700 to 1,450 B.C.E.) cities in east Crete—Gournia, Palaikastro, and Pseira—have layouts that crowded houses together, leaving little room for public squares or temples (Figure 5.1). The Minoans had no need for temples; their cults were practiced within houses and palaces, around sacred trees, or in wild surroundings. This lack of formal temples shaped the urban center into one that utilized space differently than previous civilizations. Emphasis was not put primarily on religious structures like ziggurats and pyramids; interest in developing strong city plans was often in the front of their minds. Although religious structures did play a role in the development of later Greek cities, it is clear that they never dominated the city landscape to the degree they did in previous civilizations.

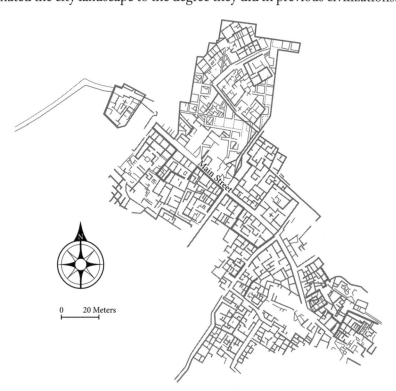

Figure 5.1 The City Plan of Palaikastro: The layout of the city of Palaikastro is an example of Minoan city planning. With the exception of a few main thoroughfares, Minoan cities were far less organized than later Greek urban sites, and were very crowded.

One of the more exciting aspects confronting someone studying Greek cities in the ancient world is their diversity. Street layout, use of walls, drainage, and placement of the agora differ from city to city. It should not be a surprise, then, to note that Greek cities during the Classical Era respond to the religious shaping of their centers in a variety of styles. One of the most famous Greek cities in the ancient world was Athens. The growth of Athens as a city was a direct result of a change in its political structure. Twelve towns in Attica, the peninsula where Athens is found, were forced into a confederation, with Athens at its head. Interestingly, although the towns were forced into this union, their religious expression did not seem hampered. Thucydides tells us that the countryside (chora) and city (polis) did not develop a sharp dividing line in politics or religion. The Greek city was not surrounded by a sacred boundary. Some of its gods had their sanctuaries in the city, others in the countryside or villages.

[handwritten margin note: Famous City]

This seemingly laid-back attitude toward sanctuary development was characteristic of the early formation of Athens. Unlike Miletus and Priene, whose development was well planned throughout every phase, Athens' growth was more organic in nature. Although the area was occupied as early as 2,800 B.C.E., the genesis of Athens is dated no earlier than 1,581 B.C.E. This date is commonly used as a point of reference, because the worship of Athena was established on the Acropolis (Figure 5.2). The Acropolis, which at first offered natural protection to early inhabitants, would evolve into one of the city's religious precincts. In Hesiod's *Works and Days*, the author recounts that most early poleis found their origin at the base of an acropolis in which geography offered easy defense. The original path that wound up the slope of the acropolis was later developed into an important commercial, civic, and religious path called the Panathenaic Way.

Later development of Athens was more rigid. An example of this more planned attempt in developing their city is best seen in the development of their port city of Piraeus. The port, which was connected with Athens by long walls, was planned by the Miletian Hippodamus, who obviously favored grid patterns. Hippodamus' plan for Piraeus is a perfect example of a planner's rational thoughts superseding the former organic growth process. There was still a religious aspect that would affect Piraeus, but on a different level. Hippodamus set land aside for sacred use, as well as public and private development. The result is that Piraeus was not a religious center that urbanized. Rather, Piraeus was an urban center that was designed with important sacred areas.

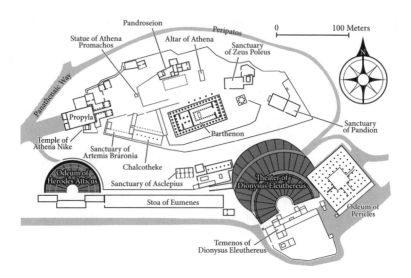

Figure 5.2 The Acropolis: The Acropolis in Athens during the time of Socrates and Plato had evolved from a defensive site to an area where many religious sanctuaries were built. The important Parthenon dominated the outcrop and the polis itself. Mythology states that once Athena defeated Poseidon, she won the right to be worshipped in that city.

Lewis Mumford, in *The City in History*, entwines Athenian religion and city further by stating that: "...Athens offers most of the ready examples of deification of the polis, the spirit itself prevailed everywhere. God, city, and citizens became one compact manifestation of ego." Mumford's assertion is that the Athenian action of raising their city to god-like status, worshipping it in a sense, led to the city being shaped in a certain fashion. Disregarding festivals and rituals that were celebrated with great regularity, citizens spent a good deal of time and money on this special urban god. More specifically, Mumford's argument compels us to consider that architectural works like the Parthenon were simply a manifestation of Athenian worship.

Temples and shrines seemed to maintain positions of prominence in cities throughout the Greek world, especially in Athens. The cities of Miletus and Priene had important temples, but these planned cities give the impression of the planner controlling the religious influence on the urban center. One point that cannot be emphasized enough when comparing the Hellenics with the Mesopotamian and Egyptian civilizations: the cities in the earlier civilizations were more heavily influenced by religion in their formation than in Greece.

Greek cities, like Mesopotamian and Egyptian cities, had economic origins that were quite alike. The Hellenic people turned to the land to develop their first economy. As Greek urban and economic history evolved, though, their cities turned more quickly from the land than did their Egyptian and Mesopotamian counterparts. Greece never abandoned agrarianism, but the very fact that they were situated on a great trade route and their population grew too large to subsist off of homegrown crops, forced leaders to make economic choices that would affect city growth. The Aegean Sea was settled by Greeks who found too many limitations on the mainland. Only in a few small patches did its land and climate combine to offer chances for mass agriculture. Cultivation was pursued by cultivating narrow strips of land which had to be dry-farmed. Few valleys ran directly to the sea, and communication between them was quite difficult. All this encouraged the residents of Attica and the Peloponnese to look outward to the sea. At the height of their civilization, no city would exist more than forty miles from the coast.

Cultivation that was pursued on mainland Greece was often done with great disregard for the future well-being of the soil. Soil exhaustion occurred as farmers continually planted the same crop, never rotating the crops or adding nutrients. The growing of wheat and barley led to farmers not having healthy harvests in Athens for a period of time. By 594 B.C.E., the crisis of land mismanagement had the city of Athens enslaving their own farming citizens for failure to repay debts. The debts were owed to aristocrats that initially lent money in exchange for one-sixth of the farmer's next harvest. Debtors made repayment virtually impossible as they planted the same crop, which failed again. Eventually, farmers used members of their family, and eventually even themselves, as collateral. The leadership of Solon, who was elected to the position of archon or ruler, saved Athens from moral and economic ruin by outlawing loans that allowed farmers to use themselves and family members as collateral. Solon also made it illegal to export those grain products that had exhausted the soil. This found planters moving away from grain altogether and moving toward the very lucrative grape and olive products. Solon encouraged others to move entirely away from tilling the soil and moved many toward the pursuit of crafts and commerce.

For a Greek citizen, commerce was not a natural path to follow. Many Greek writers record the disdain felt toward people involved in manufacturing and retail. Plato, Thucydides, Aristotle, and Xenophon all wrote about the ungentlemanly activity of trading. Yet trading along the Mediterranean was brisk. In Athens, as in most Greek cities, the agora was not only a community gathering place but a marketplace, and was central to the layout of the urban center.

The early agora was essentially a meeting place for communal activity. In some poleis, like Thera, it was nothing more than a widening of the road. The early agora was irregular in shape and use. The fact that the agora seems inconspicuous does not mean that it was not an important part of the city. It was often used to meet and discuss weighty matters of the polis. One could also find a variety of craftsmen present, but the early agora did not resemble a true marketplace. Every urban site needs to develop a meeting place where differences can be vetted out and decisions could be made; the agora was that place.

The agora, evolved from an irregular spot in a road, became more planned by the Sixth century B.C.E. By the time that the reformer Solon existed, the Ceramic Agora was deliberately laid out in Athens with a place for assembly and festivals. The Greek marketplace was a place to congregate, hear and share news, and be seen. For a people that spoke so strongly against the activity of trade, the marketplace would quickly become one of the most important sites in the city (Figure 5.3).

Trading was accomplished throughout Greece with the help of Greeks and non-Greeks who worked in cities without benefit of citizenship. These noncitizens, or metics, were important to Greek cities, playing the role of traders when Greeks found agrarianism the most important activity that one could do in life. Metics were also involved in menial labor and craftsmanship when Greeks thought that working with your hands, except when the soil was involved, was beneath them. These metics added much to the urban development of Greek cities. The majority of metics in Attica lived in Athens and especially Piraeus, which soon became the chief area of economic activity. Piraeus, which is perhaps better known as a naval base, proved to be an ideal area for commercial activity. Hippodamus of Miletus must have foreseen its possibilities, laying out two agoras when planning this town, naming one after himself (Figure 5.4). Metics flourished in Attica and left their mark in the cities where they lived. One way in which they did this was by building sanctuaries to their gods, an activity that apparently was not taken lightly by local citizens.

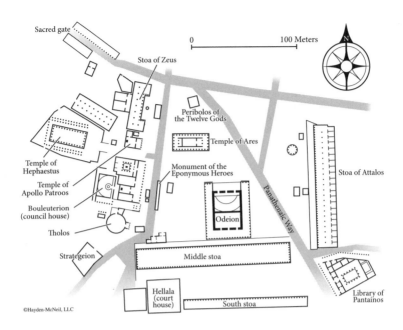

Figure 5.3 The Agora: The agora was more than a marketplace by the Sixth century B.C.E. It quickly became the most important area of the city where political, philosophical, and current events were discussed.

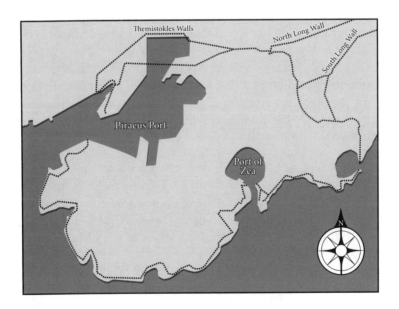

Figure 5.4 Piraeus: Probably the greatest city that Hippodamus of Miletus planned was Piraeus. Built with trade in mind, the city plan utilized its important coastline and was built with the idea of future importance and expansion in mind.

Probably the most important section of the Greek city that has economic ties is the agora. Agora is a Greek word that does not have a good translation in English. The main reason the agora was so important is because it served several functions. The agora served as a civic gathering place, but it also served as a marketplace. By the classical period, every Greek city had a clearly defined agora that was found at or near the center of the city. Athens' original agora was found on the slope of the Acropolis. By the Sixth century B.C.E. it was moved to a more central urban location. With many of the town fathers looking down their noses at the pursuits of commerce, it is ironic that the agora took such a central location in the city. Eventually commerce would become more acceptable in places like Athens. Even Solon characterizes himself as a trader in his writings. But there will exist some special circumstances, most notably Sparta, where citizens were kept from involvement in commerce. The Spartans perceived the need to build a military state, so they relied wholly on metics for commercial activity. This is not to say that the agora did not play an important role in the Spartan polis. The Spartan agora, like others found throughout Greece, became an important meeting place where politics played out and trade flourished.

Because of the economic success of Greek cities, two things happened—colonization efforts were renewed, and public works projects were undertaken. One problem that mainland Greece faced was the lack of necessary land to provide food to an ever-growing population. This was solved by several colonization efforts throughout the Mediterranean and beyond that brought Greek urban life to places as far away as the Black Sea and the south of France. This changed the shape of cities in that colonizers depopulated major urban centers in the hopes of earning wealth or land for themselves.

Also, the wealth of a given city was often reflected in the way that they displayed it through public works. Certainly the monuments built by Pericles must be linked to Athens' economic success. Some of the money can be traced to trade, some to silver that was mined at Laurion, and still more to their position as leader of the Delian League.

Many Greek cities were shaped by the need of their people to protect themselves. Foreign invasion during prehistory and the Archaic (800–480 B.C.E.) forced Hellenics to consider security first when building early urban centers. The Greeks and Egyptians obviously differed in this area, as the civilization of the Nile enjoyed a geographic seclusion

Hellenics

that minimized military considerations when building cities. Greece's topography was very different than Egypt and Mesopotamia. The same land that forced mainland Greece to look out toward the vast Mediterranean also allowed the same people to use the uneven terrain to their advantage. Early Greeks gravitated toward areas of their landscape that were easily defensible. An acropolis enabled a small army of men to ward off a large contingent of intruders. Greek cities found their origins at these strongholds that would serve both as citadels and places of worship. Athens best characterizes this scenario with a natural fortress that rose over 300 feet. The Acropolis in Athens would become the center of this great city.

With the growth of cities, Hellenic leaders considered the necessity to build walls around urban sites. The Mycenaean civilization heavily fortified themselves from as early as the Twelfth century B.C.E. Following their demise, the walling off of cities became an action that was less uniform throughout the mainland. Lewis Mumford suggests that many cities that opted not to build walls until the Fifth century B.C.E. waited because they already possessed a sense of security. Mumford infers that security was based on some form of social self-consciousness. Perhaps the explanation can be simplified. With the unusual Greek terrain working to their benefit, Greeks believed that they could rely on citadels and other unique topography in case of foreign incursion.

A foreign incursion did occur that changed the minds of most Greeks about building walls. The Persian Wars showed that the acropolis, with its varied terrain, was not enough to give protection against a large force. The Athenians watched from their island of Salamis as Athens and the acropolis were taken. When the Athenians returned to their ruined city they were faced with the task of rebuilding. Their first concern was defense. Whatever the reason for the lack of Athenian walls prior to the Persian Wars, the building of city walls now became an action that many Greek urban centers actively pursued. The archon Themistocles had long been a proponent of wall building, and it was under him that the first wall was built that encircled the city. Eventually a wall would surround both the acropolis and the city proper.

Other cities reacted to the Persian debacle in the same manner. Corinth is an example of a city that was located in a prime military location, and residents there built walls in the Fifth century B.C.E. Wall building continued throughout mainland Greece almost as a necessary part of the city. There were few exceptions to the rule. The most notable was Sparta, which preferred to defend its city behind a wall of shields. Those cities that did build walls saw significant change that altered the way they grew, for upon erecting walls choices had to be made concerning future growth. Certainly walls could be rebuilt, but walls undoubtedly retarded the growth of the urban center.

The discussion of walls in the Greek world would not be complete without referring to the "long walls" that connected Athens to Piraeus. Themistocles had once suggested moving Athens closer to the sea. This problem was solved in 461–456 B.C.E., when the Athenians built two walls from the city to the water. They enclosed her two ports, Phaleron and the peninsula of Piraeus, and afforded three harbors. Shortly after, a third wall was built to form a fortified road to Piraeus only. The Athenians hoped these walls would ensure communication with the outside world, both for commerce and naval operations. Pericles later claimed they had transformed their city from a landlocked town to a port open to the sea. The "long walls" would of course become quite handy in the First Peloponnesian War, as Pericles enclosed the citizenry within the walls and waited out their adversaries for ten years. Other mainland cities, most significantly Megara and Corinth, followed this example of wall building (Figure 5.5).

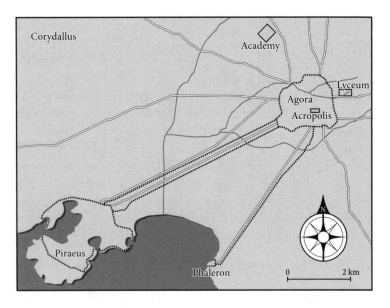

Figure 5.5 The Long Walls: The long walls connected Athens with the coastal city of Piraeus and offered them a perceived defensive advantage. The walls also helped develop Athens' trade throughout the Mediterranean, as they were no longer landlocked.

The "long wall" discussion is so important because it illustrates how a city that once was limited in its defensibility and commercial behavior was able to drastically change itself through radical urban planning. Athens had the money to build a great navy, but it was removed from a port. It had the mix of population and wealth to become a greater trading power, but was removed from direct contact to the seas. The building of the "long walls" changed all this. Although the Persian fleet would eventually find a way to block the Athenian ports and defeat them in 404 B.C.E., the transformation of Athens through this ingenuity was a high point of Greek urban planning.

The effect of militarism was significant on the shaping of the Greek urban center, but the philosophy of this civilization also had a major impact. It has been said that philosophy begins with Greece. Although this statement disregards several rich contributions prior civilizations made to this field of thought, it is true that Greek civilization was constantly teeming with new thoughts on how best to live one's life. It is not surprising to find that philosophers addressed not only how to live, be happy, approach politics, relate to gods, and commit to one another, but also how to build their cities. The three great philosophers of the Classical Era, Socrates, Plato, and Aristotle, all had opinions on urban structure. Later Hellenistic philosophers were also influential, but with a totally opposite approach. Greeks revered their thinkers, and it is apparent their thoughts were well regarded when shaping cities.

Unfortunately, Socrates wrote none of his thoughts down, but his legacy continued through some of his followers, particularly Plato. In Plato's *Republic,* Plato infers through an imaginary conversation with Socrates that unity of the state (city) is of the greatest good. So long as a city-state can grow without losing its close-knit unity, said Plato, it should be allowed to grow, but no further. Plato never would have defined Nebuchadnezzar's Babylon as a city. Plato suggested that an optimum size of a city should hover around 5,000 citizens. It is hard to believe that these two philosophers were able to exert enough influence over the Hellenic world to keep population growth down. Only three Greek cities had numbers exceeding 5,000 in the Classical world; Athens eventually had a population of 20,000. The thoughts of Socrates and Plato may not have been followed directly, but they certainly seemed to be in step with planners and city fathers of their day.

Plato's most famous student, Aristotle, had a different philosophy concerning city size and growth. Aristotle's approach to city planning was steeped in his training as a biologist. Aristotle pointed out that in every biological species there is a limit to size. Too small a village can be nothing more than a village; too large a city becomes impossible to administrate. Aristotle's reasonable argument behind city size did not fall on deaf ears. His student, Alexander the Great, had a good deal of practice in organizing cities to his likings. Seventy cities named Alexandria would sprout up through his conquests, and most had Aristotelian organization at some level. Of the seventy, Alexandria in Egypt would become the only center surviving long after the Macedonian's unexpected death. It is ironic that the city that survived would reach such an enormous size by ancient world standards. Aristotle argued against unwieldy sizes, yet Alexandria eventually reached a population of approximately one million inhabitants.

Alexander's influence on Greek cities should not be underestimated. The Macedonian's dominance over the once proud cities of mainland Greece turned them into political and social backwaters. Apparently, Alexander the Great was not only influenced by Aristotle, but also found an affinity with Diogenes the Cynic. It has been recorded that Alexander once said, "If I had not been Alexander, I should like to have been Diogenes." Diogenes' opinion toward cities was totally different than Aristotle's. Aristotle embraced the city and the social life that it offered. Diogenes advocated an ascetic life, more primitive in nature. As Alexander played the role of conqueror in Greece, he relegated cities to mere garrisons within his empire, thus changing cities as independent political bodies and curbing their ability to grow in size and influence. The Stoics, who would later streamline Diogenes' philosophy into a popular movement, emphasized an apathy that would continue to affect cities. With the Stoic philosophy of excluding oneself from political life, city growth and modernization must also have been effected. In fact, the Hellenistic Age is riddled with philosophies that counseled its followers to simply seek out personal happiness. This train of thought is the total antithesis to city and city building. Athens, Sparta, Corinth, and other Greek cities reached their pinnacle of growth and respectability through the passion filled Classical Era. They were relegated to a nation of sheepherders thereafter.

Like early civilizations, Greek cities were first established by strong-men, who established citadels. Unlike other cities of the ancient world, those early strongholds were located on natural sites that were raised above the local farming plains. These acropolises would later serve as the center of the city, with the agora, temples, residential areas, and gymnasium growing around them. Few ancient Greek cities could be termed organic. Most cities formed in a methodical and well-built manner with population, class, and commerce in mind. As well, the role of the city planners was more prominent among the Greeks than in any previous civilization.

The most significant organic city of the ancient Greek world was Athens. Although not a fully organic city, it did have a citadel and agora that must have been planned to a certain degree. It included a main thoroughfare, the Panathenaic Way, around which the city was built. And if Athens cannot be called a planned city, certainly their connecting city port, designed by Hippodamus, was the epitome of grid planning. Grid planning became more predominant in Greek cities. Hippodamus, the most influential planner of his day, designed Miletus, which featured a pattern that would survive both Hellenistic and Roman occupations of the city. Although changes were made under different ruling bodies, the remnants of the original pattern stayed in place (Figure 5.6). The rhythmic square of Miletus was strong enough to withstand centuries of change. The city of Priene and Corinth were also affected by the grid pattern. However, there were detractors to Hippodamus's style of planning. Most notable was Aristotle, who felt that it allowed invading armies too quick an advance and thieves too quick an escape.

In *Design of Cities,* Edmund Bacon points out two Greek cities that developed differently yet were still able to maintain fluidity. In the Asia Minor city of Priene, a grid plan was used to create a totally harmonious effect. Priene is an example of a planned city carried out from start to finish. Camiros, also a Greek city in Asia Minor, was rectangular and geometric. Unlike Priene, Camiros employed the talents of many designers, but had the same effect: a disciplined and visually appealing city.

CHAPTER 5   Greece

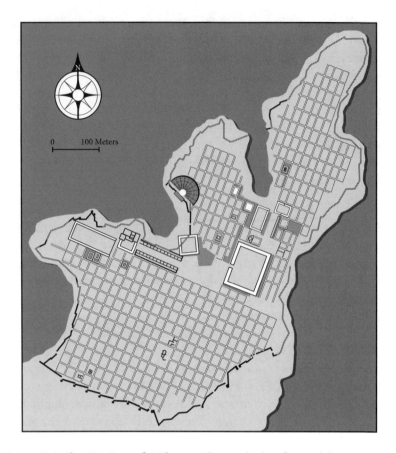

Figure 5.6 The Design of Miletus: The grid plan favored by Hippodamus is probably best seen in the design of Miletus. The flow of this pattern had positive and negative aspects, as standardization of the city could lead to ease in government but defense was questionable if the walls were broached.

• CHAPTER 6

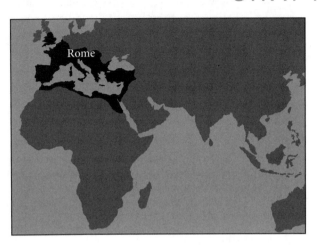

Rome

The tradition of the Roman Empire leaves the student of urban geography much to contemplate and analyze. Ancient Rome left the world with one thousand years of history, going through several phases of development. Many historians have stated that the Romans were not very original. Although it may be true that they borrowed a great deal from their Hellenic, Hellenistic, and Asiatic predecessors, they would eventually make these concepts their own. Nothing demonstrates this idea better than the Roman city.

One of the most wondrous aspects of Roman civilization was their ability to internalize other concepts that were found in lands that they conquered. Nothing demonstrates this internalization more than the effect religion had on their urban centers. It is impossible to discuss the development of Rome at any stage without pointing out the immense impact religion exerted. The foundation of Rome is shrouded in the myth of Romulus and his brother Remus. Romulus, the brother credited with the founding of the city in the Eighth century B.C.E., led a curious religious act that established the city among the seven famous hills. The act, which was Asian and Etruscan in origin, involved digging a circular ditch and replacing the soil with soil from the homelands of Romulus's comrades. This digging was believed to conjure up gods to bear witness to the founding of their new city. Although this religious rite might have taken place, it most likely did so under the earliest settlers, possibly the Etruscans, who embraced it as a necessity in founding cities.

The size of the city of Rome was governed by religious sanction. The boundary of Rome, called the pomerium, was believed to be marked by none other than Romulus. This demarcation was taken seriously, as Romulus's brother Remus would soon learn. In an attempt to mock his brother, Remus jumped over the demarcation, and as a result he was promptly put to death. This early boundary was never expanded unless further domains were added to the Roman Empire.

The Romulus and Remus myth is interesting to read, but in reality it is known that when the Etruscans arrived on the scene, there was nothing more than an array of villages among the seven hills. The Etruscans have remained a mysterious people in the sense that their origins have never been clearly identified. Several theories have arisen as to their past, but the most widely accepted places them originally in Asia. What can be said with authority is that by the Sixth century B.C.E., they had arrived in the area that would be developed by them as the city of Rome. In their wake they would leave a series of religious practices that affected the shape and growth of Rome.

What the Etruscans found among the seven hills were fortified villages. They were roughly rectangular in shape and were oriented with the long sides running north and south. The settlements were divided up into a checkerboard pattern by roads crossing at right angles. On one of the chief roads was a pit, dug for ritual purposes. There was also an arx, or citadel, and a mundus, another holy pit similar to the style that Romulus reportedly dug. This array of villages was brought under the hegemony of the Etruscans and was rapidly developed into a city.

The Etruscans did not believe that a city was properly established until it possessed three important temples honoring Jupiter, Juno, and Minerva. The three temples were built on Capitol Hill on the arx, thus becoming the Etruscan acropolis. It was important for these early settlers to have their most important gods on this height so they could overlook their city. There existed a religious ritual concerning the demarcation of the city that was similar to Romulus's alleged city boundaries. The Etruscans defined the city perimeter through the use of a white cow pulling a bronze ploughshare. The furrow was only interrupted to mark places for gates. The early act was not more than a ritual, though, because as late as the Fourth century B.C.E., when the Gauls attacked Rome, walls were limited to the arx.

The early city of Rome was axial, or symmetrical, in nature, with the cardinal points aligning with the chief streets of the future. The four sections that the city was split into were important religiously. The Etruscans were dividing the Earth like the sky was divided in Asian religions. Worship of the four winds was prevalent in East and Near East religions. In the future, this act of establishing the quadrants became so important that it was the first thing done when establishing a camp for the military. The point where the two roads met was also significant. It was at this junction that a sacred pit was established, and later the forum. The forum became the central gathering place, and political and legal business was conducted here. Temples became the most prominent landmarks in Rome over time, and they were most heavily clustered in areas like the forum, but were also in neighborhoods.

Temples made urban spaces sacred. The word *templum* did not refer primarily to the temple that sheltered a god's image. Rather, *templum* referred to a ritually defined space, set aside through sacred words and practices. The *templum* was the area where a priest stood to portion out the four quadrants of the sky. Once temples were officially established, they formed rectangular patterns enclosed with colonnades. This ritualization of space can be seen in Roman architecture and helps account for the tendency to enclose spaces.

Temples became prominent both inside and outside the pomerium of Rome because of the Romans' willingness to accept foreign gods and goddesses. Gods found their way into the city of Rome in a variety of ways. The most interesting method was when a god was formally invited. Gods were often invited to Rome and asked to leave their patron city. The perceived loss of a deity from a city meant that Rome had a better chance at being victorious over the enemy. The Roman general Scipio invited the goddess of Carthage to Rome and promptly dispatched Hannibal at the Battle of Zama. The Asiatic cult of Cybele was also introduced to the city prior to Zama and was often referred to as a leading reason for victory.

The Senate dealt with claims of divinities for recognition. The Senate was rather conservative in this area. Distinction was made between new gods and old gods and which would be allowed within the pomerium. Few gods were allowed to be worshipped in the city. The cult of Cybele was an exception, and she was enshrined on the Palatine. The Palatine Hill is the centermost of the Seven Hills of Rome and is one of the most ancient parts of the city. The origin of the word palatine is palace. It stands 120 feet above the Forum, looking down upon it on one side and upon the Circus Maximus on the other. According to Livy, after the immigration of the Sabines and Albans to Rome, the original Romans lived on the Palatine. Excavations prove that people lived on the Palatine since 1,000 B.C.E. Years later it became a place where the more affluent lived. To enshrine Cybele, a foreign god, on such an important place speaks of the importance of how religion could shape even the most important district of a Roman city.

The enshrinement of foreign gods and the maintenance of the traditional Roman pantheon were not meant to be a private manner. Roman citizens were to worship only the gods of the state. Cicero tells us, "Let no one have gods separately; nor let them cultivate in private new and strange gods unless publicly summoned." This further underscores the prominence that religion had on the city and why the urban center was dominated by temples. Rome was a city founded on religious rites and principles, and that religiosity was constantly a part of the center and the people.

Some rulers of Rome spent a good deal of time improving the city with new forums and temples. By the First century B.C.E., the old forum had become very restricted. A new forum was laid out by Julius Caesar and finished by Augustus, who built his own forum beyond it. East of these was the Temple of Peace, built by Vespasian, which was the third of the imperial forums. The relatively narrow space between the Temple of Peace and Augustus's Forum was filled by the Forum Transitorium, designed under Domitian and finished under his successor, Nerva. Finally, east of Augustus's Forum, the Forum of Trajan was built.

The rationale behind building all these forums is not entirely clear. They did not seem to have served a commercial purpose or as a place to transact legal business, as little accommodation for shade was given. Each forum did have a temple that seemed to be related to the emperor and his achievements. These new imperial forums became temple precincts that had been a feature of Hellenistic cities in the east; this idea is a fine example of Romans borrowing from the conquered.

What the people of Rome worshipped with greatest fervor was the city itself. To citizens, the state took precedent over anything else. Deification was offered to some of their leaders, most notably Julius Caesar and Augustus. Augustus was instrumental in reviving national worship among the people. As a result of municipal reorganization in 7 B.C.E., Augustus divided the city into fourteen districts and each district into fourteen wards. Each ward had an altar that honored their ruler, who gave them their prosperity. So Augustus not only secured his power over the people of the city, he developed a new administrative style by portioning off the city into areas that were easily handled (Figure 6.1).

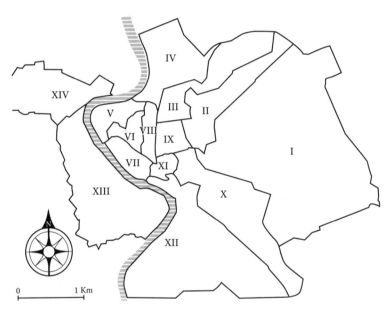

Figure 6.1 Augustus Divides the City of Rome: Augustus secured his power effectively by dividing the city into fourteen districts. Each district was divided into fourteen wards.

Religious influence over the city of Rome was completed with the introduction of the one faith that would entirely dominate the empire, Christianity. The god of the Christians would not be accepted readily into the Roman pantheon, primarily because the faith was monotheistic, thus excluding all other state gods from worship. Later effect on the city can be examined when speaking of the long-term impact of Christianity. Certainly the building of churches changed the texture of the urban center. More important than the building of churches and eventual dominance of Rome by the Vatican itself is the attitude that early founders had toward the city and civic life. What was so dangerous to Roman leaders about Christianity was that it operated outside the confines of the state. Christianity ended the connection between the state and religion in Rome that gave the governing class so much power. Membership in the church became a spiritual matter and had nothing to do with nationality. The god of the Christians had no obligation to protect one people from another. As well, Christianity worked well in urban areas, where its message toward the meek, poor, and disenfranchised found a large audience.

As Christianity became more successful, two things happened. Some of the best minds of the city retreated from urban life to seek answers in monastic orders. Monasticism required men to devote their life to God and remove themselves from the world to contemplate weighty spiritual matters. This was a drain on city life. More importantly, the widespread acceptance of Christianity moved men away from the idea that civic life came first. Christianity contributed to Rome's downfall, as it was no longer the cohesive body it once was. Christianity should be added to the long list of reasons the Roman Empire fell in the west. Alaric's ease in sacking Rome in 410 C.E. has often been pointed to as being the primary cause of the fall of the western Roman Empire. But one should add the success of Christianity to any list of causes. In effect, Christianity assisted Alaric in changing the shape of Rome in 410 C.E. by making the cities less unified.

Another aspect that helped shape the city of Rome and other urban centers in the empire was its economy. Like civilizations that came before, Romans would turn to agriculture as their primary industry. One must note that the land of Italy did not offer many resources to exploit, other than its fertile soil. Because of these conditions, the people that lived in the area of what would later become Rome became adept agrarianists. Their ancestors would remain long after an empire arrived on the scene. When the Etruscans arrived on the scene, the people they encountered made their living primarily as farmers. As the city crystallized under these new people, the agrarian lifestyle continued to dominate.

One way in which the agrarian economy shaped Roman cities was the way in which the countryside was perceived. In ancient Rome, most of the countryside belonged to one city or another. City territories were of substantial size, and their rural inhabitants counted as part of the city. Secondary towns were developed in these territories where farmers could live away from the land. This phenomenon of so many farmers living away from the primary urban center must have relaxed many population pressures. It allowed the center to grow at a steadier pace, if it grew at all.

With the passing of the Seventh century B.C.E., many important events changed the course of Italian commerce. Phoenician trade diminished rapidly, partly because of Assyrian pressure in Syria. Greek trade was increasing, and Syracuse now controlled the Sicilian Straits. At this time, the Etruscans became more dominant in the land of Latium, where Rome and its surrounding countryside lay. With a strong command of the Tiber River, Rome was tied to the Mediterranean Sea trade. The initial connection did not mean that the city became a great commercial center overnight. In fact, during the Etruscan period, international trade was minimal at best.

As Rome grew, so did trade. The response to trade would indeed shape the cities of the empire. At its height, the city of Rome held 1,200,000 people, a number too large to feed and service with Roman staples. As foreign trade became more and more necessary, the way in which commerce was conducted changed. The most apparent physical changes that took place were the building of necessary harbors and harbor cities. Rome is set back along the Tiber River, and for captains of ships the river presented many dangers. The resolution to this problem was the building of artificial ports. Two ports that were built to address this problem were Ostia under Claudius (r. 42–54 C.E.) and Portus under Trajan (r. 100–106 C.E.) (Figure 6.2). Once docked, goods were unloaded from various ships and stored in warehouses.

Ostia had been in existence since the middle of the Fourth century B.C.E. as a military colony. When Claudius built the artificial harbor, it was transformed into the most important port in the Roman Empire. The most important cargo of Ostia was grain. In the harbor of Ostia, the grain was transported onto barges for immediate shipment upstream to Rome. The harbor city of Ostia reached a population of 60,000, a considerable size in the ancient world.

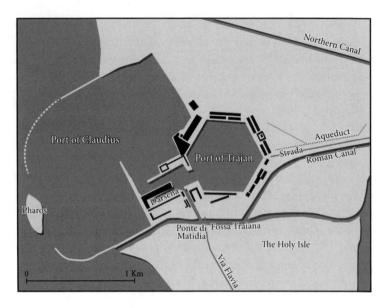

Figure 6.2 The Ports of Ostia and Portus: As the population of Rome grew, the need to service Rome became more important. Rome's original harbor was Ostia, developed by Claudius and enlarged by Trajan. The first Portus site was built by Claudius and was approximately 180 acres. Further inland, Trajan built the hexagonal port, which was approximately 100 acres. Both artificial harbors were built to meet the needs of the burgeoning population.

The earliest traceable settlement at Ostia was a rectangular castrum of about 5.5 acres. A castrum is a plot of land set aside to build defensive positions. At Ostia, two streets crossed at the center, where presumably the forum was located. To the east, one of these streets continued toward Rome, via Ostiensis. To the west, it split in two just outside the castrum gate. One road led to the mouth of the Tiber; the other to the seashore. The harbor city grew considerably in the Second century B.C.E. Houses, temples, and a new set of walls increased the size of the city. By the time of Augustus, Ostia became a boom town (Figure 6.3).

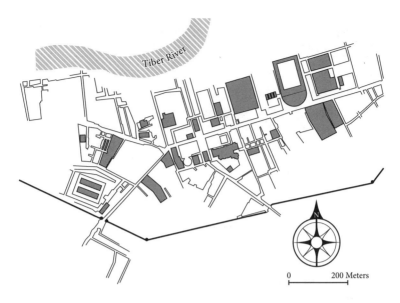

Figure 6.3 Ostia: The image of Ostia during the time of Augustus articulates an urban center that was thriving. With a large population for the ancient world, it developed all the accoutrements that any Roman city might have during this period. Temples, markets, and forums were all prevalent in this urban site, which was planned using the castra template.

It was important politically to obtain cheap food for the poor. With over one million people living in the city, this made a place like Ostia both an economically and politically important city. Each month, about 1,200,000 modii of wheat (over 300,000 bushels) were distributed to those on the dole. The government also had to keep a fair amount around for other citizens and for the population of Ostia. To meet such needs, Egypt sent an annual shipment of 20,000,000 modii and Africa about 40,000,000 modii. In all, approximately 15,000,000 bushels each year were sent to Rome via Ostia. Just the shipment of grain should underscore the importance and growth of this city, whose raison d'etre was to service the city of Rome.

Romans were urbanites. Nothing characterizes this more than the way in which victorious Roman legions dealt with foreign lands and people. Although this will be discussed later in this chapter, it would be wrong not to point out how the Romans used economics to shape colonial cities. The trend of urban life was deliberately fostered in backward areas by the Roman government. The intent of building things such as markets, houses, and temples was to lure barbaric people away from their patterns of existence. The marketplace, or agora, dominated these cities, offering them the best products of the empire and assisting in the Romanization of the so-called barbarians.

Most markets, whether in colonial cities or out, were often grand architectural compositions. The market seems to have been built more with civic pride in mind than anything else. A letter from the council of Hermopolis to Demetrius, controller of the market, is significant: "The civic market is an ornament of the city and contributes little profit." Economy helped shape ornamental features in Roman cities, tame barbarians, and develop areas like Ostia and Rome into major cities.

Romans are probably less remembered for their economy than their military might, and it is very true that this factor played a tremendous role in shaping not only the city of Rome but also other cities it founded or changed after conquering. In fact, it can be said that after the Romans developed their city, they went to great lengths to create images of that city elsewhere. This change of urban form around the Mediterranean and beyond not only changed the shape of the city, but it created a different culture. Municipal towns built on the Roman template would shape the urban experience throughout the Roman world.

In order to impose and maintain their authority throughout their empire, the Romans established a practice of town planning that was military in origin. The Romans built thousands of fortified legionary camps known as castra, which were meant as temporary centers for military activities. The legion's first goal when developing the encampment was to build it as quickly as possible. To achieve this goal, strict rules applied to all castra. Each castrum was laid out according to a gridiron within predetermined rectilinear perimeters. Though castra were initially meant to be temporary, a large number later formed the basis of permanent towns that would evolve into cities.

Permanent settlements, whether evolving from military camps or not, emulated the design of the castra to offer simple and standardized urban planning. The perimeter was usually square or rectangular; within, two main cross streets formed the basis of the street structure—the decumanus, through the center of the town, and the cardo, usually bisecting the decumanus at right angles toward one end. Secondary streets completed the grid layout and formed the building blocks, known as the insulae. The forum area, the Roman equivalent of the agora, was typically located in one of the angles formed by the intersection of the cardo and decumanus. That forum normally had a meeting hall constructed at one end with a colonnaded courtyard (Figure 6.4).

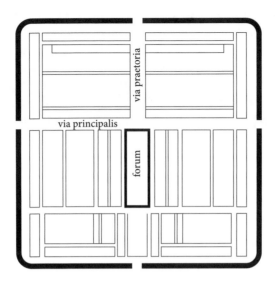

Figure 6.4 The Castra: Above is an example of a Roman Castrum. The via praetoria, or cardo, ran north and south and intersected with the via principalis, or decumanus, that ran east and west. Near the intersection, the forum was built.

The layout of the castrum and development of Roman wall building was important and played a lead role in drawing the outline of the city. It must be remembered that initially, the rectilinear city finds its origin in the religious. Later, the rectangle form is kept as the castra that were built for every overnight camp that a Roman legion built. Although the design is the foundation for civil towns, this is not to say that civil towns were built in the exact layout of a castrum. If the site of the castrum was to be reused as a civil town, the military buildings and streets were completely cleared away to facilitate the building of the new town. Sometimes, the area occupied was that of the castrum and its original walls were retained. The castrum almost always generated marketplace trade and the total conversion to civilian occupation often took the form of a military nucleus, with an organic town growing around the military camp.

There are many good examples of castra evolving into cities in the Roman Empire, but nothing gives a better example of this military influence than Corinium, Londinium, and Timgad. Corinium, modern-day Cirencester, evolved out of a large castrum of about 30 acres that housed a half legion of 3,000 infantry. At the time it was founded in 43–44 C.E., it controlled an important intersection. Over the next twenty years, a street grid was laid out and the town was furnished with an array of large public stone buildings, two marketplaces, and numerous shops and private houses. Development continued until the Fourth century C.E. Part of the reason that the Romans developed a castrum in Corinium is that three main Roman roads met in this area, underscoring the importance of the town. These were the Fosse Way, Akeman Street, and Ermin Street. In the Fourth century the town became the capital of the new province Britannia Prima (Figure 6.5).

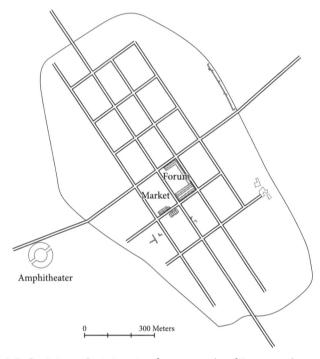

Figure 6.5 Corinium: Corinium is a fine example of Roman urban planning being used in important frontier towns. Notice the street grid layout that is still prevalent in modern-day Cirencester, England.

Whereas scholars agree as to the fact that Corinium was founded using the castrum form that later evolved into a city, Londinium's beginnings are far less clear. Londinium, modern-day London, was founded about seven years after the Romans invaded Britannia in 43 C.E. Unlike other examples of a castrum forming first and a civilian town forming later, Londinium had some civilian settlement present prior to Roman invasion. Once a Roman military presence was born, a small area was developed near the Thames River, with the design used throughout the empire. Although the city suffered a setback when the Celtic queen Boudica and her men burned it down in 60 C.E., by the next decade it had recovered and continued to expand. By the Second century, Londinium had grown so exponentially that it became the new capital of Britannia for the Romans. Its population would reach 60,000 inhabitants. It featured major buildings including bath houses, an amphitheater, and a city garrison (Figure 6.6).

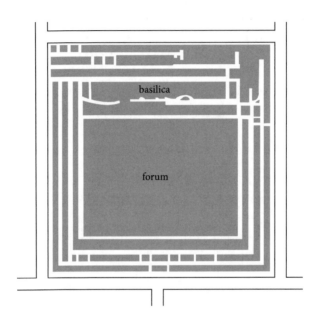

Figure 6.6 Londinium: Although there were settlements near modern-day London when the Romans arrived on the scene, formal city planning took place using the castrum template once the area was settled by the Empire.

A phenomenon of note regarding these frontier villages is that legion veterans often found their retirement homes outside the walls of the garrison. This would be a natural occurrence for a soldier spending any period of time stationed in some frontier area like Asia Minor, Africa, or Gaul. Interaction with locals often led to marriage and settling in the area outside the original castrum or within the civilian town, if one took root on its foundation. With the settlement of retired legionnaires, the Roman Empire enjoyed a population that would help Romanize the foreign residents and assist the standing force in times of need.

A well-preserved legionary town that historians are quite knowledgeable about is the North African town of Timgad, found in modern-day Algeria. Timgad was founded in 100 C.E. by the Emperor Trajan for veterans of the Third Legion, which garrisoned in the nearby fortress of Lambeisis. Upon completion, the town was almost square with sides of about 380 yards. Timgad was a relatively small city, planned and built quickly with the simplicity found among other frontier towns in the empire. It initially was intended to provide accommodation for 15,000, but it soon outgrew that number and moved beyond the original grid. The initial plan of Timgad featured a regular checkerboard layout with facilities one would expect in any Roman city: colonnaded walks, forums, a theater, an arena, baths, and public latrines. As the plan quadrupled over the next 300 years, new quarters had to be made. Outside the original perimeter, organic growth added to its size in a suburban environment (Figure 6.7).

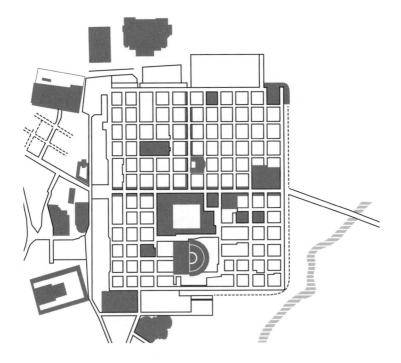

Figure 6.7 Timgad: The city of Timgad reflects the classic Roman design of urban sites in frontiers. It is also a perfect example of a site that remained so popular that urban sprawl took place around the original plan, as can be seen in the illustration.

Timgad stood, as did other cities in the empire, as a clear expression of Roman power. Each site used a solid and brilliantly conceived plan that was executed well by positioning the site near an important headwater or confluence of trade routes. These Roman cities relied heavily on the castrum plan for development and emphasized the importance of militarism on urban planning throughout this civilization.

With the enormous amount of land that the Roman Empire conquered, it is important to note that there was never a city as significant as Rome until Byzantium arrived on the scene. This was an intended consequence of the empire not allowing a center to grow so large that it might challenge them in the future. Several cities like Rome could have formed, but the constant dispersal of people throughout the empire allowed a single city to remain preeminent and residents to shape new sites as they saw fit.

Where militarism may have played a significant role in shaping the urban form, the most popular philosophies of the day had less to offer. The leading philosophy in Rome was Stoicism, which was adopted from the Hellenistic Greeks. Stoic philosophy was very agreeable to Roman life, in that the philosophy accepted all situations. Whether a situation was good or bad, passive acceptance of life was necessary. Philosophically, Romans considered their crowning achievement to be *virtus*, meaning "manliness" or "toughness." This concept of *virtus* was a crucial component for a political career. Its broad definition led to it being used to describe a number of qualities that the Roman people idealized in their leaders.

Virtus was often associated with aggressive behavior that manifested itself by supporting a conquering emperor, general, and army. The very idea that this concept existed as a part of a dominant part of the major philosophy assisted in the growth of the empire. With that growth, Romans developed their cities in such a way that expressed their *virtus*, or, in this case, control over a specific region. The city, evolved from the castrum, was a testimony to their *virtus*. So important was the concept of *virtus* that soldiers were unable to take the field of battle unless they gained permission from their general. This also kept the army in strict order.

The centerpiece of Stoic philosophy was the concept of the *logos*. The Romans believed that the universe was ordered by God and this order is the *logos*, which means rational order of the universe. Stoics felt that the *logos* of each individual life, action, and situation was determined by its place in a larger whole. In understanding this concept, one might understand how the empire developed cities as just a smaller part of the whole, cogs in the greater machine that was Rome. Imagine a far-flung empire, held together by a great road system connecting organized cities with the major urban center of Rome. This in many ways expressed the great order found in Stoic philosophy.

For the Romans, this philosophy revealed itself as their common law spread across the world. Stoicism allowed the Romans to shape the cities not only through *virtus* but through their common law. In order to spread this common law into cities, the development of urban sites that would remind the conquered of Rome and its greatness were necessary. The spread of Rome meant the spread of her laws, and nothing expressed this better than the Roman city.

The Roman city was influenced by the many factors that have been previously discussed, but it is always worth mentioning the impact of planners on its shape. Unlike other civilizations previously discussed, it is difficult to point out unique Roman planners throughout its history. There is no doubt that the Greek planner Hippodamus of Miletus gave Romans many ideas for the planning of their own cities and the development of established cities, but singular names do not stand out in this field.

Archaeology tells us that the western half of the Roman Empire and many districts in its eastern half used a definite town plan, which can be best described as a chessboard pattern. As mentioned previously, the tie to religion and later the military laid the foundation for its development. The decumanus and the cardo, the two main lines of the Roman land survey and probably also the two main streets of the Roman town plan, were laid out under definite semireligious provisions. A system of town planning that is so distinctive and so widely used might reasonably have created a series of building laws sanctioning or modifying it. This did not occur. Neither the lawyers nor even the land surveyors, the so-called Gromatici, tell us of any legal rules relative to town planning as distinct from surveying in general. The surveyors, in particular, are much more concerned with the soil of the province and its limitation than with the arrangements of any individual town, and throw no light on streets and insulae.

The nearest approach to building laws that occurs is a clause that seems to be a standing provision in many municipal charters, and similar documents from the age of Cicero onward, to the effect that no man might destroy, unroof, or dismantle an urban building unless he was ready to replace it by a building at least as good or had received special permission from his local town council. The earliest example of this provision occurs in the charter of the municipality of Tarentum, which was drawn up in the time of Cicero. It is repeated in practically the same words in the charter of the colony Genetiva in southern Spain, which was founded in 44 B.C.E.; it recurs in the charter granted to the municipality of Malaga, also in southern Spain, about 82 C.E. Somewhat similar prohibitions of the removal of even old and worth-less houses without special leave are implied in decrees of the Roman Senate passed in 44 C.E. and 56 C.E., though these seem to relate to rural rather than to urban buildings. Hadrian, in a dispatch written in 127 C.E. to an eastern town that had recently obtained something like municipal status, includes a provision that a house in the town belonging to one Claudius Socrates must either be repaired by him or handed over to some other citizen. Similar legislation occurs in 224 C.E. and in the time of Diocletian and later.

Rules were also laid down occasionally to forbid balconies and similar structures that might impede the light and air in narrow streets, and it was a common rule that cemeteries and brickyards must lie outside the area of inhabitation. In Rome, too, efforts were made by various emperors to limit the height of the large tenement houses. These limits were, however, fixed haphazardly without due reference to the width of the streets; they do not seem to occur outside of Rome, and even in Rome they were very scantily observed.

But in general, no definite laws were framed. It is likely the municipalities were somewhat closely tied in the administration of municipal property and had to refer to schemes for the employment even of the smallest bit of vacant space to the patron or the curator of the town. But, apart from the provisions mentioned previously, they had no specific rights that are recorded against private owners or builders. It was only once, after Rome itself had been burnt down, that an imperial order condemned landowners who held up their ground instead of using it, to forfeit their ownership in favor of anyone who offered to build at once.

It is clear that if any planning was taking place, the government of Rome throughout history played that major role. Although they were influenced by the Greeks and Etruscans early on, the Romans developed their own super-planning committee that micromanaged the urban site, particularly outside of Rome itself. Conclusively, the major imprint on the urban center was the military, which was initially influenced by religious practices that may have dated as far back as the Neolithic Age.

CHAPTER 7

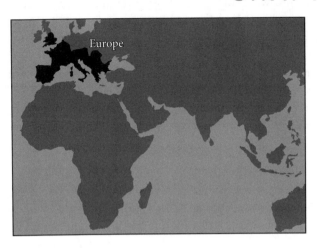

Europe

The study of European cities is very different than any previous area discussed. Europe developed its urban centers after a good deal of influence from earlier civilizations. So when we discuss the shaping of their urban forms, we must relate it back to previous civilizations. Early influence in southern Europe can be tied directly to the Phoenicians, who transmitted their culture throughout the Mediterranean. Later, the Greeks would push their way as far west as modern France to establish colonies. Colonization would take place in both the Seventh and Tenth centuries B.C.E. With the eventual rise of the Roman Empire, new cultural influences entered the area of Europe and affected its urban growth. As well, the dominance of Muslim Empires, particularly the Umayyad Caliphate on the Iberian Peninsula, would be of importance. The history of urban centers in Europe is more complex than in previous civilizations because Europe was affected by so many diverse groups. The end result is that many of these cities maintained remnants from earlier contacts and thus developed unique living spaces for Europeans. Before the Greek and Roman civilizations, it is impossible to characterize Europe as urban. The area was dominated by semi-nomadic people who settled in villages, but certainly nothing as advanced as cities. These "barbaric people," as the Greeks termed them, were influenced by the Druidic religion that was extended to Britain. Julius Caesar wrote that the religion would not foster the need for an immediate political union. Caesar's argument about Druidism was that it may have existed prior to Roman dominance, but its effect on urbanism was negligible.

Urban centers grew when the Greeks first entered the area and exerted influence. The year 600 B.C.E. marks the foundation of the Greek colony Massilia (modern Marseille) by the Phocaeans. Phocaea was a minor eastern Greek city now in Turkey that, fearing foreign domination, sought new colonies throughout the Mediterranean, with cities in southern Italy, Corsica, and northeast Spain, as well as Marseille. The early European city is a fine example of Greek influence in the region. Strabo, in his *Geography*, describes Marseille in detail and gives readers an idea how Greek culture and religion shaped this center (Figure 7.1):

> Marseille, found by the Phocaeans, is built in a stony region. Its harbor lies beneath a rock, which is shaped like a theatre and looks towards the south. It is well surrounded with walls, as well as the whole city, which is of considerable size. Within the citadel are placed the Ephesium and the temple of the Delphian Apollo. This latter temple is common to all the Ionians; the Ephesium is the temple consecrated to Diana of Ephesus. They say that when the Phocaeans were about to quit their country, an oracle commanded them to take from Diana Ephesus a conductor for their voyage. On arriving at Ephesus they therefore inquired how they might be able to obtain from the goddess what was enjoined them. The goddess appeared to them in a dream to Aristarcha, one of the most honourable women of the city, and commanded her to accompany the Phocaeans, and to take with her a plan of the temple and statues. These things being performed, and the colony being settled, the Phocaeans built a temple, and evinced their great respect for Aristarcha by making her a priestess.

Unfortunately, many aspects of Massilia city life are unknown, even after excavations. But there is enough written documentation to gain a general feel of the importance of religion in the development of this city. Temples of Artemis and Apollo are mentioned in historical sources as well; the previously mentioned religious sites that Strabo wrote about leads scholars to believe that Gallic Greek urban centers shared much with other Greek cities. Temples and shrines seemed to maintain positions of prominence throughout the Greek world. Lewis Mumford adds, "In the smaller towns like Marseille, Narbonne, or Orange in southern France, with their independent foundations in Hellenic (Greek) culture dating back many centuries, the Greek tradition must have dominated both politically and architecturally."

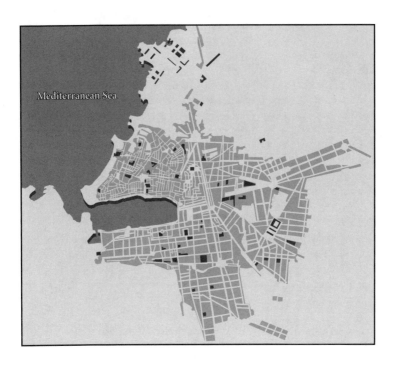

Figure 7.1 Massilia: Massilia, modern-day Marseille, was founded by the Phocaeans from Asia Minor. The city commanded an important port that made them successful in trade along the Mediterranean.

Europe transformed into a more urbanized era during the ancient world once the Romans expanded their empire north and west. Religion had an enormous impact on the development of cities in Romanized Europe. The very shape and size of the urban centers were controlled by religious sanction. Cities were, with few exceptions, axial in nature. Two major streets were laid out in every urban setting that symbolized the way in which their Etruscan predecessors believed the earth and sky were separated. The point where the two roads met was significant because early on this was the place where a ritual pit was dug. Later, this would become the site for the forum. The forum became the central gathering place for individuals and it would become a place where legal and political business was transacted. Temples became the most prominent landmarks in Roman cities over time; most were clustered in areas like the forum as well as neighborhoods (Figure 7.2). As well, this axial, rectilinear way of building cities became convenient for conquerors to quickly lay out a multitude of urban centers throughout Europe.

CHAPTER 7 Europe

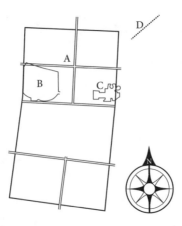

Figure 7.2 The Roman Forum: In cities that were founded by Romans in Europe, the forum became a central area where all important matters were discussed. Above is a diagram of Lindum, modern-day Lincoln. A denotes the location of the forum, B was a former Norman castle, C was where a cathedral was built, and D was a known route of an aqueduct.

When Christianity burst onto the scene, it was merely a cult following. In time, though, the small reform movement would dominate the European landscape and leave a lasting impression on its urban centers. By the time of the Middle Ages, the Christian Church had become the force that held civilization together in cities. Its preeminence would naturally set the tone for urban growth. A.E.J. Morris states in his book *History of Urban Form* that the space that lay in front of the church, the medieval parvis, should not be confused with the burial ground that might adjoin the church as seen in Britain. The parvis was a gathering place for the faithful where events like mystery plays may take place. From the Twelfth century on, the west portal of the church was the normal gathering place for such activities.

Occasionally, sermons and processions passed through this area, celebrating important religious holidays and venerating particular saints that may have been important to that particular church and congregants. The parvis was also the place where the faithful gathered before and after services. People from out of town left their horses and soon stalls of various kinds were set up. Nonetheless, the parvis was never intended to compete with the market square. The parvis, or in Britain, the burial ground, meant that churches were generally located within their own space. As this frequently adjoined the market square, a two-part nucleus is a typical characteristic of medieval towns, both planned and unplanned (Figure 7.3).

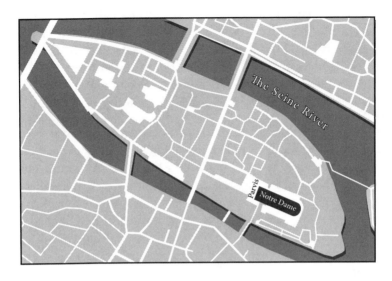

Figure 7.3 The Parvis: The above illustrates the Place du parvis Notre-Dame in Paris. This parvis is a perfect example of one that was used in the variety of activities mentioned. The parvis still sees celebrations for St. Mary in the month of May, but it has become much more sedate in the modern era.

Church was not an activity simply set aside for Sabbath or other holy days. The Church dominated many aspects of the average person's life. Even in a small village, hundreds of clerics lived and watched after the spirituality of the masses. Cathedrals were so large that entire populations could worship together. As well, pilgrimages to cities were common when the bones or relics of a saint were purported to be held at a church or monastery. Vezelay, France, grew simply on the religious distinction that the bones of Mary Magdalene laid at rest in its Benedictine Abbey. The yearly pilgrimages, and the town's growth, ended when the relics were found to be at another city.

Other church-related buildings, such as poorhouses and hospitals, were built throughout the urban centers. Widespread building of monasteries also took place during the Middle Ages. All of this building reinforced the dominance of the Church in European cities. Christianity was not the only major religion in Europe, though, and there were other religions that assisted in developing the center from a religious perspective. On the Iberian Peninsula, Islam penetrated Europe and made lasting impressions on the urban landscape. Around 711 C.E., Muslim forces crossed the Straits of Gibraltar and occupied southern Spain. The Visigoth Kingdom, already weakened by internal warfare, quickly collapsed, and by 725 C.E. most of the Iberian Peninsula had become a Muslim state with its center in Andalusia. Seven years later, an Arab force, making a foray into France, was defeated by the army of Charles Martel at the Battle of Tours. The Muslim forces were pushed south over the Pyrenees Mountains and settled in to rule the area that we know as large parts of Spain and Portugal today.

Like the Christian cities to the north, places of worship dominated urban centers in the Iberian Peninsula. One of the greatest cities that developed under Umayyad influence in Spain was Cordoba. Cordoba was the heart of Islamic Spain, and the heart of Cordoba was the Great Mosque. Around it sprang up the schools and the markets with their shops. At its height, the population numbered eighty thousand and was quite prosperous. Cordoba developed a prototype for future Islamic cities in the region, with its narrow alleys crisscrossing and running at random, incidentally providing shade from the beating of the sun. In fact, the only part of Islamic towns endowed with squares and streets large enough for commercial and social activities was the mosque-market area.

Religion influenced the development of urban centers in Europe, from early Greek contact throughout Christian and Muslim periods. The positioning of places of worship, be they temples, mosques, or cathedrals, often characterized the shape of the city. If a city was important enough to have a bishop living within it, the building of walls around ecclesiastical castles might also take place. In time, the Roman Catholic Church would become one of the great landholders in the West, and with that distinction came power. Eventually, it claimed much of the power over urban growth.

Prior to Greek contact with Europe, economics in this area was similar to other preceding civilizations around the world. The semi-nomadic people of Europe turned to subsistence agrarian lifestyles in order to maintain themselves. Just as the Mesopotamians, Egyptians, Greeks, Chinese, and Romans had sought fertile land near rivers and waterways to settle and farm, so too would early Europeans first make their mark. Because of this simplistic way of life, nothing more than villages dotted the landscape, and it would be impossible to argue that urbanization was the result of agrarianism in ancient Europe.

City life arrived in Europe with colonization. The Phoenicians, who lived in the area of Palestine along the Mediterranean, became international sea traders after the fall of the Hittite Empire in 1,200 B.C.E. Trade was the Phoenician occupation, and it did not require settlement overseas. Yet they came to base themselves more and more in colonies and trading stations. In the end, there were some twenty-five Phoenician settlements throughout the Mediterranean, the earliest set up at Kition in Cyprus at the end of the Ninth century B.C.E. Some colonies may have followed earlier Phoenician commercial activity. They may also reflect the time of troubles that overtook the Phoenician cities after a brief phase of independence at the beginning of the first millennium. In the Seventh century B.C.E., the Phoenician city of Sidon on the shoreline of the eastern Mediterranean was razed to the ground, and the daughters of the King were carried off by the Assyrians. Phoenicia, after the rise of the Assyrians, was reduced to its colonies throughout the Mediterranean and little else. They must also have been anxious about the wave of Greek colonization taking place at the same time in the Mediterranean. This could explain the Phoenician founding of the city of Carthage a century earlier. The end result was that the Phoenicians established a number of colonies throughout Ancient Europe, southern Spain, Sicily, and Sardinia. These important colonies would lead to early development of urban centers in areas that had not yet realized urbanization.

Although the Phoenicians made their presence known in early Europe, other civilizations would also be driven to colonize in the area. The Greeks would send two large waves of people throughout the Mediterranean to colonize. Colonization for the Greeks was motivated less by trade than by the basic need to address the problems that were associated with overpopulation. Traditionally, Greeks felt that the finest way that a man could earn a living was by working the soil. So much did they support this idea that foreigners, called metics, were once recruited to work as menial laborers and craftsmen. Settlements in Italy and Gaul were found as favorable sites. Syracuse and Catania were Greek settlements in Sicily, Croton and Caere were settled on mainland Italy, and Massilia proved to be an important port in Gaul (Figure 7.4).

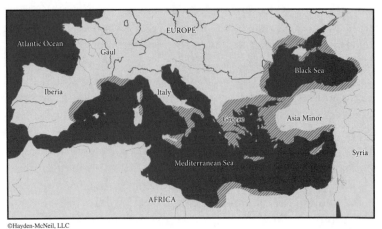

©Hayden-McNeil, LLC

Figure 7.4 Greek Colonization: Two waves of Greek colonization took place in the Mediterranean. By 550 B.C.E., important areas of southern Europe were being influenced by these people.

Sicily was one of the richest of the areas colonized by the Greeks. A fertile soil with good rainfall produced enough wheat and corn to feed much of Greece. From ca. 735 B.C.E. on, the Greeks poured in and founded the urban centers of Naxos, Syracuse, Leontini, Messana (Messina), Catania, Gela, Himera, Selinus, and Acragas. In all these cases the natives were driven from the coast by force of arms. Most of them retired to the hills to till the land in the mountainous interior. Some became slaves, but so many others intermarried with the conquerors that Greek blood, character, and morals in Sicily took on a perceptible native tint.

The most important city in Sicily was Syracuse. As far back as the Eighth century B.C.E., the Greek polis Corinth had sent colonists to seize the little peninsula, which was perhaps an island. They built or widened the connection with the mainland of Sicily and drove most of the natives into the interior. They multiplied with the rapidity of a vigorous people on a resourceful soil. In time, their city became the largest in Greece, with a circumference of fourteen miles and a population of a half million people. Greek settlement in Syracuse was a perfect example of an urban setting growing due to economics. Syracuse was a success because their agrarian business and trade made them successful.

On mainland Italy, Greeks made inroads and set up important colonies whose sole reason to exist seemed to be trade. Croton developed on the Tarentine Gulf, across the heel of the peninsula. Trade between eastern Greece and western Italy had a choice of two routes: one by water and the other, in part, by land. Ships following the water route touched at Croton and exchanged many goods there; from there, they could pass through the Messina Straits and on to the northernmost Greek settlements in Italy. The voyage past Croton was quite dangerous, as the seas were ridden with pirates. This led to the second route that led through Sybaris, another Greek settlement in Italy. Rather than go through the dangerous Messina Straits, merchants could unload their goods and have them carried across land. The result was that Sybaris prospered until it had a population of 300,000 and gained a wealth few Greek cities could match. All physical labor was performed by servants, and any noisy labor was not allowed in the city. Ironically, the ultimate demise of Sybaris would come at the hands of Croton after a brief war. Nevertheless, both cities characterize how economics played such a large role in the development of cities in early Europe.

In Gaul, the oldest urban center was established at Massilia (Marseille). The attraction to the area was obvious with its fine harbor. Founded by Asiatic Greeks from Phocaea in about 600 B.C.E., it made its money from seaborne commerce, the transit trade, and commissions. Because it was established on a peninsula, the layout of the city is irregular with a labyrinth of dark, steep streets. It took advantage of an acropolis to develop the necessary religious site that Greek poleis offered.

Massilia became so prosperous that its economic dominance spread along the coast in both directions. Nice, Antibes, and Olbia owed their existence to the city. Olbia had a grid-like pattern of streets with a multitude of warehouses to accommodate its vigorous commerce. Because Massilia traded with Spain, Italy, Sardinia, Corsica, and Carthage, hoards of coins show that she played a part in the economic development of the Rhone valley.

It is perhaps too difficult to make general comments concerning how the Greeks in early Europe affected the shape of cities through economics. The Greeks brought with them the concept of the agora, thus making it a part of their new cities. But one must keep in mind that all of these new cities that were mentioned were successful because, for one reason or another, they were economically successful. Trade and agrarianism helped the Greeks introduce their own brand of urbanization to the Europeans. The real story is that urbanization, spurred on by economics, reached this area.

If the Greeks seemed a bit inconsistent in the shaping of their cities in any uniform manner, their successors, the Romans, made up for any deficiency. The Roman influence in Europe would far exceed any other civilization's previous contact. The Romans entered Europe and established themselves not only militarily, but also economically.

Julius Caesar's success in conquering Gaul in 58–51 B.C.E. allowed the Romans to enter modern-day France and Germany and change the lifestyle in which these peoples lived. Caesar's subsequent victories in England extended the Empire's control further north and west than it had ever been. One of the first things that armies attempting to subjugate an area must do is create supply routes. Rome would develop a myriad of routes that led to the development of a corridor along the Rhone, Saone, Moselle, and Rhine Valleys as the main economic axis of Gaul and Germany. One of the major cities in the corridor was Lyon, which was situated at the confluence of the Rhone and the Saone Rivers. It was a point at which goods were shipped and traded.

When Caesar first encountered Gaul, the only cities to speak of were in the south and had been established centuries earlier by the Greeks. Caesar came into contact primarily with villages throughout Gaul, but once routes were established for his army, many villages benefited from being conquered. The next major towns were Metz, then Trier and Cologne, or Mainz. All had significant communities of merchants, and acted as redistribution centers for trade in their respective regions. These villages that would later form into cities took on the shape of many of the Roman urban centers. The Romans built many centers using the basic castrum layout that was reminiscent of legionnaire camps. This was difficult to do with an already established site that had been growing organically over the years.

In some cases, natives would settle near the outside of forts to take advantage of trade and other possible service industries that a Roman camp may establish. There are examples of these camps becoming major cities. Two good examples of this would be London and Colchester. Colchester was built quickly by direct imperial orders for retired legionnaires. When the legionnaires arrived in 43 C.E., the locals were allowed to stay, although a fortress was established half a mile away to keep a watchful eye on the people. A small fort was also placed two miles away, where there was a pre-Roman religious center. The Romans still allowed locals to congregate there and after a period of seven years demilitarized the area and created a colonia (Figure 7.5).

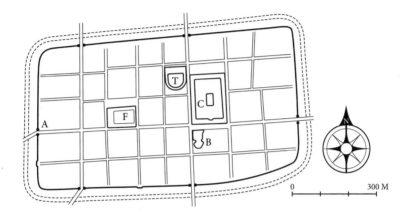

Figure 7.5 Colchester: Camulodum (Colchester) was one of the earliest and most rectilinear Romano-British towns. The following is a key to the above map: A, the main gateway to town (from Londinium); F, forum; T, Theater; C, Temple of Claudius; B, baths.

There was no evidence of permanent settlement prior to the Romans conquering the area we now call London in 43 C.E., but by 70 C.E. Tacitus called it a city "thronging with businessmen and merchants." From 44–50 C.E. roads and buildings were laid out on a regular plan, probably military in nature. A military post and a bridge over the Thames were built during this time period. The next ten years saw much re-planning and development: timber-framed houses with clay floors and plastered walls, and even piped water along the main road. This growth was more civilian than military in nature and probably reflects commercial exploitation at the site, both for trade in general and as a center for supplies for the armies fighting in the north. Docks, too, must have been developed. Thus, London soon superseded Colchester, which had been the main trading center. Its location on the Thames must have also been more convenient than Colchester's location on the Colne (Figure 7.6).

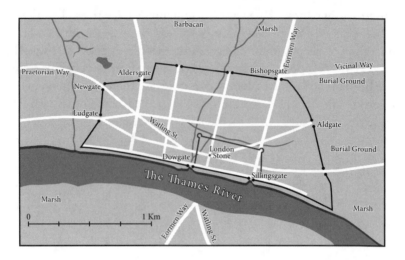

Figure 7.6 London on the Thames: The location of London on the River Thames made the site an important business metropolis.

Agriculture, though, would remain the fundamental industry for the Europeans throughout the Roman times. The Romans, no doubt, transformed the entire area with their policy of urbanization, but the life of the towns depended on farmers. Mining also proved to be a new form of economy that entered into the area on a large scale. Caesar mentioned bronze, tin, gold, and iron in relation to Britain. Coal, tin, and iron were mined on a considerable scale, but they, like agriculture, did little to shape the urban landscape.

On the last day of December 406 C.E., a large number of Alans, Vandals, and Sueves crossed the frozen Rhine into Roman territory. If any date can be taken to mark the end of Roman Europe, this one has the best claim, for the region would never be the same again. Despite the continuation of some form of Roman rule up to 486 C.E., the Fifth century was a period of political and cultural turmoil. There is little trace of Romanized life continuing after the first decade of the century, with the major exception of the Church. The decline in urban centers and countryside would take place. At the same time, coin use came to an effective end, pottery production virtually ceased, and there were hardly any secular building projects.

The fall of the Roman Empire and their eventual loss of control of the European landscape would change how the urban center was developed economically. Although agrarianism remained the mainstay of European economics, trade would remain important. This would change with the rise of Islam throughout the Mediterranean. Islam would at one time control Northern Africa, the Iberian peninsula, and Palestine. By the Eighth century European trade was cut off in the Mediterranean. The Ninth century European urbanites would feel the wrath of the Norse so severely that by the end of the century, any serious commerce had disappeared. The disappearance of any significant commercial life led to the downfall of the city in Europe.

Although Europe experienced a decline in urbanization in the Ninth century, the following century would reestablish the urban center throughout the landscape. Europe would look into itself and establish trade routes that helped revive old cities and develop new ones. Europe would have to wait until the founding of the Hanseatic League, in the city of Lübeck, which developed a trade system throughout much of northern Europe in the Thirteenth to the Seventeenth centuries.

The city of Ghent is a prime example of an urban center flourishing due to commerce. During the Norse invasions, the local nobility had built fortifications against future attacks at the confluence of the Lieve and the Lys Rivers. Prior to 100 C.E., across from the river to the south, a commercial center called the poertus was established. By the end of the Twelfth century it had grown substantially and was surrounded by walls. Within another 100 years, more land was annexed and more fortifications built. Other Flemish sites would follow in Ghent's path and some new centers would develop as well. A commercial revival recreated Ghent.

Other cities would grow with the economic revolution that struck Europe. Along the Rhine, no city could have been more important in the Twelfth century than Cologne. At Cologne, an area called the Rheinvorstadt, which included a market and wharves, developed between the river and the original city. By the Twelfth century three extensive suburbs were formed, then enclosed. Cologne would become the primary trading city along the Rhine River. Imperial edicts even indicated that nothing traveling west, east, or north could pass by the city (Figure 7.7).

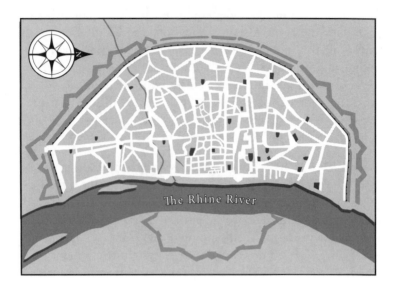

Figure 7.7 Cologne: Straddling the Rhine River and a major imperial road, Cologne evolved into an important trade city in Europe.

It is easy to be misled that the revitalization in commerce was the only thing that sparked the growth of cities in the Middle Ages. One must not forget that Europe had an agrarian-based economy and would maintain it until the Twentieth century. But that is not to say that agrarianism did not help urbanization. The Middle Ages produced a curious political and economic system called feudalism. Feudalism was a system that involved a large landholder, commonly referred to as a lord, who entered an agreement with lesser landholders called vassals. In exchange for a variety of things such as protection, these vassals paid tribute or provided troops to the lord. As well, these vassals had their own vassals. The whole system was based on the ownership and working of the land. The person on the bottom of this economic food chain was the peasant. The importance of feudalism to the revitalization of urbanism is that it provided surplus food for the cities so urban centers could continue to grow.

The street systems in medieval cities were closely related to economic activities. Trade and production took place throughout the center, with a premium on street frontage. Passages were made for easy access from street to street, and pavement in many major cities became necessary. The formal market could be found at a variety of places, depending on how the city grew. There was the traditional square, often found in or near the city center. The second type of market was one that occupied a widening in the street (Figure 7.8).

Market Hill

Figure 7.8 The Medieval Market: Medieval markets were often no more than a widened street, as can be seen in the illustration. Formal markets were more common in larger cities.

The European economy declined between the Fourteenth and Eighteenth century because of a variety of problems. Shortage of money constantly threatened trade and the city's life. The return on profits in farming was not as great as it should have been, largely due to the fact that techniques did not keep pace with the need for more surpluses. Fortunately, overseas expansion and colonization abroad would give the necessary economic boost to cities, particularly port cities in Europe.

The influence of militarism on European cities is similar to the influence that militarism had on urban centers in previous civilizations. The primary reason this is true is because cities did not evolve until their cultures came into contact with other civilizations. The Phoenician, Greek, Roman, and Arabic civilizations would bring their own unique views on how militarism should shape the cities. The Greeks would introduce walls and the Romans would develop the castrum; in the end, the Europeans would bring their own brand of militarism to bear on the shape of the city.

Prior to the Greeks arriving on the European scene, the Phoenicians would develop colonies throughout the Mediterranean. The Phoenicians, who made a name for themselves as commercial traders, also built fortified cities in Spain. From their base in Carthage, other sites,

CHAPTER 7 Europe

including Cadiz, New Carthage, and Saguntum, were developed. The principle aim of Carthaginian colonization, apart from commercial development, was to acquire men for their army and gold for their treasury. The Carthaginians greatly forwarded public works, constructing palaces, forts, and roads. Often these ancestors of the Phoenicians are remembered simply as great traders and innovators of language. But one must not forget that they also fought the Romans in two major wars. Their cities reflected the fact that they were a powerhouse.

The Greeks were the next civilization to leave a lasting impact on the European urban scene. The Hellenics sought out new places to live partly for commercial reasons, but largely because of population problems at home. Once they settled, all of their cities were influenced by militarism. Because land was at a premium in the Greek world, defense of that land was also important. Sicily, southern Italy, and southern France all saw the development of Greek urban settlements, and thus the effects of militarism.

The oldest Greek presence in Europe and oldest French city could be found in Massilia (Marseille). The obvious attraction to this area is that it offers a fine harbor for a commercial people. The Asiatic Greeks, the Phocaeans, created this city around 600 B.C.E. Both Marseille and a site called St. Blaise left a unique new dimension to the city—the wall. Built of carefully squared blocks fitted together without mortar, they rose from twenty feet in height to thirty at the towers, and were seven to twelve feet thick. Their footings go down to the bedrock. Within the walls there is evidence of a gridded street plan and sidewalks.

In terms of militaristic influence, all other civilizations pale in comparison to the Romans. Certainly the Romans were interested in trade, just as the Phoenicians and Greeks before them, but they seemed to measure the entire success of their civilization by their military. It is not a surprise, then, to notice that city development for the Romans was a reflection of their military spirit.

The standard layout of Roman cities in Europe evolved from the way in which legionnaire camps were laid out. It was important to lay out standard camps that were easily defensible and quick to put together when Roman soldiers were on the march. Rome built thousands of fortified camps known as castra that featured a rectilinear layout with two major streets: the decumanus that ran through the center of the town and the cardo that bisected the decumanus at right angles. Secondary streets completed the grid layout and formed the building blocks known as the insulae.

One classic example of the castra being used for colonies in Europe would be Gloucester, England. Initially a legionary fortress, Gloucester was eventually built into a colonia. The legionary barracks were demolished. Their place was taken by buildings that closely resembled them in plan. You can superimpose the colonia on top of the original legionary fortress and notice that very few changes were made (Figure 7.9). This example of castra being used throughout Europe as a layout to later build Roman colonies and cities became the standard.

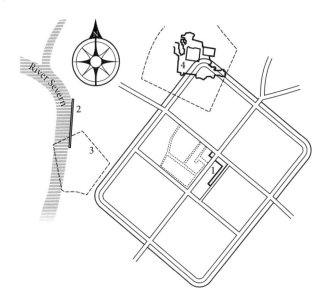

Figure 7.9 Gloucester: Gloucester was built on the right bank of the Severn and was founded for veterans. It was built about half a mile from a legionary fortress. The following is the key to the map: 1, forum; 2, Roman quayside; 3, first army fort; 4, medieval cathedral.

With the fall of the Romans, the people of Europe were left to their own devices to either perpetuate cities along the same method that the Romans had offered or add their own militaristic influences. Without the Romans as a unifying force, a good deal of in-fighting occurred amongst Europeans for land rights and general supremacy over the area. One example of a city in Europe growing after Roman domination had passed was Leichester. The Romans had developed Leichester in the standard layout that has been discussed. It became less important once the Romans disappeared, but would again gain notoriety after the Norman Conquest. King William ordered a castle to be built and the population increased. Its walls followed the Roman antecedents, with four gates and two roads bisecting in the center (Figure 7.10).

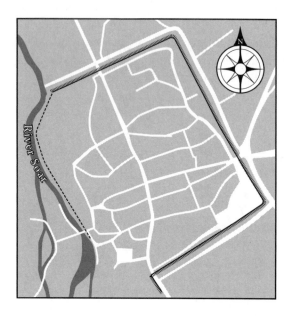

Figure 7.10 Leichester: Sitting on the Soar River, Leichester was developed as a standard Roman city.

One of the most distinctive elements of town design was the perimeter. Most centers had an easily recognizable outline created by their fortifications, gates, and towers. The earliest such constructions of earth and timber were replaced by heavy stone walls, particularly in the period between 1,100 and 1,500 C.E., when methods of warfare became more sophisticated. As wealthier towns grew more land was enclosed, so the walls were not perceived as a permanent barrier. The citizens and rulers of Paris constructed five walls between 1,180 and 1,845 C.E., as the city continued expansion. Only a few cities in Europe did not have walls.

As Europe evolved from earliest urbanization to 1,500 C.E., militarism seemed constant on the city dwellers mind. The idea of a wall was something that virtually every city dweller wanted not only for peace of mind, but for a sense of community. Although post-Roman Europeans enjoyed the idea of having fortifications they were not as happy with the presence of a castle in their city, because it often reminded them of subjugation. Not all nobility were looked upon as benevolent masters.

Although militarism was important in forming the European city, the philosophy that was transported from other civilizations also played a crucial role in its shape. By 600 B.C.E., Europe was beginning to be influenced by city builders from Greece. The Greeks that brought the polis to the south of France would also bring their brand of philosophy to the area—a philosophy of individual freedom. This did not mean that the freedom of organic cities was introduced alongside them. Like most cities that developed after conquest, grid plans were often laid out.

Spiro Kostof points out in *The City Shaped: Urban Patterns and Meanings through History:*

> "The Greeks seem to have latched on to the grid in their colonizing efforts as early as the 7th century B.C. Colony is apoike in Greek, an emigration, an "away home," not a mere tributary like the modern colonial cities of the Western powers. If there was an increase in an urban population beyond what the countryside bear, a colony was sent out. So Corinth spawned Syracuse in Sicily, and Syracuse spawned Acrae and Camarina in an ever westward expansion. The population of these cities was usually small, about 5,000. By 600 B.C., in the western Mediterranean, Greece was colonizing what are now southern France, Sicily, and southern Italy, Libya and Spain. Here, in the colonies, there was no Greek village structure that had to be respected, no ancient Greek sanctities."

Therefore, there was no justification for the making of "organic" cities. This was historically done in ancient Greece through the joining together of several towns to form a single community. Assimilation was unnecessary in the eyes of Greek colonists. Prior land division did not have to be respected. In the colonies, the land was culturally and ritually blank—from the Greek point of view, of course. They brought their gods and their cults, and institutions like the agora—that premier symbol of self-governance—and the concept of the polis itself.

Greeks, Kostof seems to be intimating, transplanted their philosophy of the city that was developed partly through great philosophers like Socrates, Plato, and Aristotle. All three men represented the thinking of Hellenics when they expressed the point that there was no better way to live than as a member of a polis. Aristotle claims, after deep pondering, that if a person does not want to be a part of a polis it is only because of two things: they are a god or a beast. All great thinkers of the day felt that organized life for all men began in the city. The necessity of its organization beyond its homeland was apparent.

The Romans followed the Greeks as the great urban center shapers in Europe. The Roman philosophy behind shaping cities was less esoteric than the Greeks. The Roman urban sites were, almost without exception, rectilinear with a grid street layout. The developing of cities in this manner was probably more a result of the fact that these ancestors of Romulus were trying to maintain a military presence in the area and build an empire. Grid-like systems can serve many purposes—one is controlling a hostile group around you. Another point that might be overlooked in the building of early Roman sites is the statement that these centers make to the people being subjugated. Julius Caesar was famous for impressing his Gallic enemies by building bridges over large rivers in a day and then not using them to advance his troops. Caesar's statement was, "Look at the power of Rome, and look at our ability!" The brisk building of sites must also have been equally impressive to a non-urban people.

As the city passes in to the Middle Ages in Europe, one thing can be said: the growth of cities throughout Europe would be inconsistent. Unplanned towns grew around marketplaces, a castle, a church, monastery, or a mixture of these. Former Roman towns developed in other places. And where population in some English sites barely reached 5,000, other places like Venice reached 50,000. There was only one single common denominator during this period: the Church.

The diffusion of the Church through the Roman world in the Fourth century took place largely through the conversion of the urban lower and middle classes. And the world of the Catholic Church became significantly more urban in the Middle Ages. Monastic houses that had originally been in the countryside were engulfed by expanding cities. Canon law provided that bishops lived in cities, and new orders like the Dominicans and Franciscans found their work in the cities. The existence of the Church often revitalized towns and made some cities important places of pilgrimages where cottage industries evolved. Churches often became the center of towns, with streets radiating out from them. The importance of the Church in some cities will remain to the present day.

The interest in Europe was initially found to be among people interested in commercial interests. Massilia, Saguntum, New Carthage, and Cadiz were all early cities founded with trade on the minds of the inhabitants. Certainly the planners looked out toward the Mediterranean when they were laying out the cities.

Success in commerce often led to cities evolving into a city planned by different people. Massilia is a good example of a city that is established first as a trading post and colony; later it will be known as a powerful military city that establishes other sites for itself. This change in raison d'etre must have also changed the form of the city. Better walls must have been established to guard them from future foreign incursions. They will eventually fall to Rome, only after defying them on several occasions.

In discussing the role of strongmen as planners, one must examine the role of the Romans in European city planning. The Romans felt that they had the art of urban site building down to a science—so much so that the names of people that helped in laying out significant sites remain anonymous. The most we can gather is that there were professionals in every legion whose job was to lay out encampments after long marches. These people were often used when laying out sites for legionnaires to retire to in Europe. These sites are still a part of many well-known European cities today.

The Middle Ages felt the effect of planning through local nobles who were increasing their power and protecting themselves by building castles and walls. People gravitated toward this protection against the nomadic Huns and Vikings. Walls would not only be an issue that nobility sought, but in cities that were not dominated by a lord, walls would also be built. Some cities did not need strongmen in the Middle Ages; they had successful merchants. Merchants in many cities played a major role in the planning and expansion of the urban center as they developed ports, market areas, walls, and civic areas. The city of Cologne would be a perfect example of this form of planning being controlled by the populace.

CHAPTER 7 Europe

●— Bibliography

Chapter One

Bacon, Edmund. 1976. *The Design of Cities.* Penguin Books.

Bottéro, Jean. 1992. *Mesopotamia: Writing Reasoning, and the Gods.* The University of Chicago Press.

Kostof, Spiro. 1992. *The City Assembled: The Elements of Urban Form Through History.* Bulfinch Press.

Kostof, Spiro. 1991. *The City Shaped: Urban Patterns and Meanings Through History.* Bulfinch Press.

Kramer, Samuel N. 1963. *The Sumerians.* The University of Chicago Press.

Morris, A. E. J. 1972. *History of Urban Form.* George Goodwin, LTD.

Mumford, Lewis. 1961. *The City in History.* Harcourt, Brace & World.

Oppenheimer, A. Leo. 1977. *Ancient Mesopotamia: Portrait of a Dead Civilization.* The University of Chicago Press.

Roberts, J. M. 1993. *The History of the World.* Oxford University Press.

Von Soden, Wolfram. 1994. *The Ancient Orient: An Introduction to the Study of the Ancient Near East.* William B. Eerdmans Publishing Co.

Weber, Max. 1958. *The City.* The Free Press.

Wiseman, D. J. 1983. *Nebuchadrezzar and Babylon.* Oxford University Press.

Woolley, C. Leonard. 1965. *The Sumerians.* W. W. Norton.

Chapter Two

Bacon, Edmund. 1976. *The Design of Cities*. Penguin Books.

Kostof, Spiro. 1992. *The City Assembled: The Elements of Urban Form Through History*. Bulfinch Press.

Kostof, Spiro. 1991. *The City Shaped: Urban Patterns and Meanings Through History*. Bulfinch Press.

Mumford, Lewis. 1961. *The City in History*. Harcourt, Brace & World.

Robins, Gay. 2000. *The Art of Ancient Egypt*. Harvard University Press.

Silverman, David P. (Editor). 1997. *Ancient Egypt*. Oxford University Press.

Chapter Three

Bacon, Edmund. 1976. *The Design of Cities*. Penguin Books.

Kenoyer, Jonathon Mark. 1998. *Ancient Cities of the Indus Civilization*. Oxford University Press.

Kostof, Spiro. 1992. *The City Assembled: The Elements of Urban Form Through History*. Bulfinch Press.

Kostof, Spiro. 1991. *The City Shaped: Urban Patterns and Meanings Through History*. Bulfinch Press.

McIntosh, Jane R. 2008. *The Ancient Indus Valley: New Perspectives*. ABC-CLIO, Inc.

Mumford, Lewis. 1961. *The City in History*. Harcourt, Brace & World.

Possehl, Gregory L. 2002. *The Indus Civilization: A Contemporary Perspective*. Rowman & Littlefield Publishers, Inc.

Wright, Rita P. 2010. *The Ancient Indus: Urbanism, Economy, and Society*. Cambridge University Press.

Chapter Four

Bacon, Edmund. 1976. *The Design of Cities*. Penguin Books.

Bai, Yunxiang. 2009. *On the Early City and the Beginning of the State in Ancient China*. Bureau of International Cooperation, Hongkong, Macao and Taiwan Academic Affairs Office. Chinese Academy of Social Sciences.

He, Congrong. 2007. *Architecture of Xia, Shang, Zhou Dynasties and Spring and Autumn Period.* CORE OCW.

Kostof, Spiro. 1992. *The City Assembled: The Elements of Urban Form Through History.* Bulfinch Press.

Kostof, Spiro. 1991. *The City Shaped: Urban Patterns and Meanings Through History.* Bulfinch Press.

Li, Liu. 2004. *The Chinese Neolithic: Trajectories to Early States.* Cambridge University Press.

Mumford, Lewis. 1961. *The City in History.* Harcourt, Brace & World.

Needham, Joseph. 1959. *Science and Civilisation in China.* Cambridge University Press.

Siren, Osvald. 1926. *The Imperial Palaces of Peking.* AMS Press.

Chapter Five

Bacon, Edmund. 1976. *The Design of Cities.* Penguin Books.

Bayhan, Suzan. 2002. *Priene, Miletus, Didyma.* Keskin Color Kartpostalcilik Ltd.

Connolly, Peter and Dodge, Hazel. 2000. *The Ancient City: Life in Classical Athens and Rome.* Oxford University Press.

Gates, Charles. 2011. *Ancient Cities: The Archaeology of Urban Life in the Ancient Near East and Egypt, Greece and Rome.* Routledge.

Homer. Trans. by Fagles, Robert. 1990. *The Iliad.* The Penguin Group.

Kostof, Spiro. 1992. *The City Assembled: The Elements of Urban Form Through History.* Bulfinch Press.

Kostof, Spiro. 1991. *The City Shaped: Urban Patterns and Meanings Through History.* Bulfinch Press.

Mumford, Lewis. 1961. *The City in History.* Harcourt, Brace & World.

Owens, E. J. 1992. *The City in the Greek and Roman World.* Routledge.

Ward-Perkins, J. B. 1974. *Cities of Ancient Greece and Italy; Planning in Classical Antiquity.* George Braziller.

Wycherley, R. E. 1976. *How the Greeks Built Cities: The Relationships of Architecture and Town Planning to Everyday Life in Ancient Greece.* Norton Library.

Chapter Six

Bacon, Edmund. 1976. *The Design of Cities.* Penguin Books.

Connolly, Peter and Dodge, Hazel. 2000. *The Ancient City: Life in Classical Athens and Rome.* Oxford University Press.

Gates, Charles. 2011. *Ancient Cities: The Archaeology of Urban Life in the Ancient Near East and Egypt, Greece and Rome.* Routledge.

Kostof, Spiro. 1992. *The City Assembled: The Elements of Urban Form Through History.* Bulfinch Press.

Kostof, Spiro. 1991. *The City Shaped: Urban Patterns and Meanings Through History.* Bulfinch Press.

Mumford, Lewis. 1961. *The City in History.* Harcourt, Brace & World.

Owens, E. J. 1992. *The City in the Greek and Roman World.* Routledge.

Chapter Seven

Bacon, Edmund. 1976. *The Design of Cities.* Penguin Books.

Braunfels, Wolfgang. 1990. *Urban Design in Western Europe: Regime and Architecture, 900–1900.* The University of Chicago Press.

Kostof, Spiro. 1992. *The City Assembled: The Elements of Urban Form Through History.* Bulfinch Press.

Kostof, Spiro. 1991. *The City Shaped: Urban Patterns and Meanings Through History.* Bulfinch Press.

Mumford, Lewis. 1961. *The City in History.* Harcourt, Brace & World.